ALL YOU NEED TO KNOW ABOUT THE BIBLE

Book 2:
big claims from a unique book

BRIAN H EDWARDS

DayOne

© Day One Publications 2017

ISBN 978-1-84625-585-4

All Scripture quotations, unless stated otherwise, are from The Holy Bible, New International Version Copyright © 1973, 1978, 1984 International Bible Society

British Library Cataloguing in Publication Data available

Published by Day One Publications
Ryelands Road, Leominster, HR6 8NZ
Telephone 01568 613 740   Fax 01568 611 473
North America Toll Free 888 329 6630
email—sales@dayone.co.uk
web site—www.dayone.co.uk

Cover design by Kathryn Chedgzoy
Printed by T J International

ALL YOU NEED TO KNOW ABOUT THE BIBLE

BRIAN H EDWARDS

Book 2
Big claims
from a unique book

The series outline

Book 3 Have we got the right books?

1. Who thought of a Bible?
The idea of a collection of books

2. The Jews and their Bible
The books in the Old Testament

3. The early Christians and their Bible
The beginning of a New Testament

4. A growing collection
The development of the accepted books

5. A complete New Testament
The books accepted across the Christian world

6. Who wrote the books?
The writers of the New Testament books

7. Helpful letters not in the Bible
More instructions for the young churches

8. A library of lies
The writings of the heretics

Appendix
A chart of the church Fathers

Book 4 A journey from then to now

1. From flames to fame
The story of the English Bible

2. How old is the Old Testament?
The earliest copies

3. How old is the New Testament?
The earliest copies

4. Discovering the best text
Why are some verses different?

5. Which translation?
The dilemma of many versions

Book 5 Sense as well as faith

1. Tearing the Bible apart
The Bible and its critics

2. Great minds on a great book
What scholars say

3. Digging up the evidence
Archaeology confirms the truth

4. Guidelines for combat
Errors and contradictions?

5. Solving the problems
Resolving some of the issues

Book 6 Enjoy your Bible!

1. It's for you, it's alive—read it!
The best way to read the Bible

2. Reading the Bible with common sense
A guide to a good understanding

3. A bit more common sense
Types, symbols and dangers to avoid

4. Getting to grips with the Old Testament
A chart of the books in their proper place

5. Piecing the Gospels together
A harmony of the life of Jesus

6. Where did they write their letters?
The Acts of the Apostles and where all the letters fit in

7. Reading the Bible from cover to cover
A careful plan to read it all in eighteen months!

8. Take time with God
Spending time each day with God

Contents

What this book is all about

The human race should know how to live and how to get the best from life. With our superior intelligence and power of reason and conscience, should be able to chart a reliable course for peace, harmony and good-will for the benefit of all. However, this optimistic hope is clearly ill-founded.

So what went wrong? When Adam and Even disobeyed the command of God, rebellion against the Creator entered the whole of human nature. The Christian Bible reveals God's master-plan of how the human race should live, can live, and one day will live when God recreates everything new. All this, and much more, was the subject of Book 1. The purpose of this second book is to affirm the authority and accuracy of the Bible, and how we can confidently reach this conclusion. The first thing that is essential when anyone begins to read the Bible is to know what it claims for itself.

God has revealed himself in many ways throughout history and especially through Jesus Christ. However, the particular reference in this book is the truth that he has given in the revelation of Scripture. We focus on what is really meant by the words 'inspiration' and 'inerrancy' and why it is so important, and correct, to defend these claims from the text of the Bible itself. A careful definition of how the Scriptures came to us distinguishes a true belief in biblical authority from more vague or rigid ideas. Importantly, a survey of the long history of a belief in Biblical inerrancy shows that this vital truth has always been the position of the greatest theologians of past centuries.

The third and fourth chapters, discuss how Jesus and the apostles used the Hebrew Scriptures (our Old Testament), and why they were often using a Greek translation rather than the Hebrew Old Testament. We may also be surprised at how frequently the apostles used the Old Testament in their writing—clearly for them, the New did not dispense with the Old. The Old Testament prophets, Jesus himself and the apostles, each made uncompromising claims for the absolute authority of both the Old Testament Scriptures and their own words. Were they right? And do they each agree with one another? When Jesus affirmed, 'the Scriptures cannot be broken' (John 10:35), he clearly meant much more than we often realise.

Chapter 6 answers the question: Is the Bible enough? Can anything be added to it, or is it sufficient and final? What do we mean when we speak of the sufficiency of Scripture? Does it tell us everything we need to know about everything, or only everything we need to know about some things? These are all questions that need to be carefully unravelled so that we don't fall into the danger of making claims that are either too general or too restrictive.

In the 1970s, when the debate about Biblical inerrancy was probably at its most intense, the International Council for Biblical Inerrancy was formed. After ten years of meticulous scholarship, vigorous debate, and many publications, their excellent legacy is still with us. This second book in the series closes with their careful and valuable statement set out in nineteen points on what evangelicals really mean by Biblical inerrancy.

However, can we be sure that we have the right books in our Bible? That is the subject of Book 3.

1. The God who reveals himself

God has revealed himself in many ways throughout the history of the human race. He has also left clear instructions for us.

Almost everything that is manufactured comes with a set of instructions. We call these 'the maker's instructions'; the more complex the item, the more detailed is the information. We may choose to ignore the maker's instructions, but if we do, then we cannot blame the manufacturer when things go wrong. If they are not obeyed, then the product may be damaged and will not function properly.

It is reasonable to expect that if there is a God who made everything, he must know best how it should all work. It is also reasonable to assume that he will have given instructions, and that those instructions will be reliable. For the most complex part of his creation—which is us—we would expect the most detailed information. Contradictory instructions would be absurd, therefore we cannot claim that all religious books will be equally helpful in locating the truth about life, death and eternity because they each have very different messages.

Something went wrong

We might expect that the human race would know how to live and how to get the best from life. Birds and animals know how to migrate and look after their young, and nobody gives them a set of written instructions. Humanity, with its superior intelligence and power of reason, should be able to chart a reliable course for peace, harmony and good-will for the benefit of all who live on this small but well-provided-for planet.

Unlike the birds and animals, people—all people—have a sense that some things are right and some things are wrong; we call this a moral consciousness. Philosophers debate where this came from, but the Christian believes that it was given by God when he marked out the human race as his special creation. However, our optimistic hope is clearly ill-founded, because humanity has not made a good job of managing planet earth over the past millennia. In a fallen world, we can still see the imprint of God's order, design, and beauty, but the order and design are broken, beauty is tarnished, harmony is shattered, joy is compromised and God's bountiful provision is manipulated by the human race to its own destruction.

SO, WHAT WENT WRONG?

In Genesis 1–3 the Bible relates how God created the first man and woman and they entered into a relationship of friendship with their Creator that was not shared with any part of the animal kingdom. With the natural creation, God coded into the genetic makeup of each part the information that was essential for success in survival. But with mankind he added to all this a personal relationship with himself that involved communication and instruction. Unfortunately, the first significant instruction was disobeyed and from there everything went wrong.

The immediate result of this 'Fall' was that the special relationship was marred and Adam and Eve wanted to avoid God and what he had to say to them (Genesis 3:8). From now on the human race refused to listen to God and turned its back on him. Because of that first rebellion, a curtain was drawn across the mind of everyone, and all generations from Adam have been in mutiny against God's best plans for creation to such an extent that they are ignorant of the Maker's instructions. As a storm cloud hides the clear brightness of the sun, so rebellion causes men and women to lose sight of God; consequently they lose their way in life. The Bible calls it a spiritual blindness (2 Corinthians 4:4), and elsewhere it is referred to as a spiritual darkness (Colossians 1:13;1 Peter 2:9). The repercussions of this refusal to listen to God is that humanity manages to spoil almost everything good that God has made.

The clearest picture of the condition of our present world is found in Romans 1:18–32, which begins by describing,

'... all the godlessness and wickedness of men who suppress the truth by their wickedness, since what may be known about God is plain to them, because God has made it plain to them. For since the creation of the world God's invisible qualities— his eternal power and divine nature—have been clearly seen, being understood from what has been made, so that men are without excuse.'

That is the result of ignoring the Maker's instructions. God might have left the human race entirely to its own ignorance and self-destruction, but he chose not to. Instead, he left sufficient evidence of himself all around us in the world, and planned also to make two specific forms of evidence more clear than anything else—and we will come to those shortly. It is sufficient to say that if humanity is to know anything about God then it must be God who takes the first step. He must draw back the curtain, remove the thick cloud, and reveal himself and his will in clear and unmistakable ways.

The word 'revelation' comes from a Latin word *revelatio*, which means 'to make something known that is hidden'. We dispel the darkness and uncover that which is hidden. Most important of all is the fact that when we talk of God's revelation we mean that God reveals *himself* to us. It is not simply God revealing how he acts, or what he thinks; still less is it just a matter of God telling us how he wants us to act and think. All this is important, but most important of all, revelation is God showing us who he is. He reveals that he is the eternal Creator who is holy, just and good, and hates sin—yet will, and does, have mercy upon the entire human race even in its rebellion. Therefore, the Bible is first and foremost a book about God. We must never forget this.

The purpose of God revealing himself to men and women is to restore them to true fellowship with himself. Revelation is God reaching into our darkness to show us the truth about himself in order that we might come to love, worship and obey him. Revelation must therefore be true and reliable, or else it is meaningless.

God's general revelation

Although God hates sin, he has mercy upon the entire human race even in its rebellion. There is a general revelation, sometimes called 'natural revelation', which is available for everyone both to see and enjoy. Not all will see it with understanding, but all will enjoy it to different degrees. This is also known as God's universal grace. No one will have any excuse for ignoring it, because God has made it plain. General revelation comes to us in at least three ways.

REVELATION IN NATURE

In the Old Testament, we read of David who, before becoming king in Israel, spent his youthful years as a shepherd and later as an outlaw. He lived in the desert and was constantly trying to escape the army of King Saul. David often walked out into the hills alone and looked up into the sky. There, in the sun, moon and stars, he could see the work of a great God. In one of his many psalms he wrote:

'The heavens declare the glory of God; the skies proclaim the work of his hands. Day after day they pour forth speech; night after night they display knowledge. There is no speech or language where their voice is not heard. Their voice goes out into all the earth, their words to the ends of the world' (Psalm 19:1–4).

Elsewhere the psalmist poetically thought of the whole creation having a voice that gives praise to its Creator:

'Let the sea resound, and everything in it, the world, and all who live in it. Let the rivers clap their hands, let the mountains sing together for joy; let them sing before the Lord' (Psalm 98:8–9).

The whole world can hear this voice and see this picture. No one is excused for not listening and looking—and then worshipping. This revelation in nature speaks about humanity also:

'When I consider your heavens, the work of your fingers, the moon and the stars, which you have set in place, what is man that you are mindful of him, the son of man that you care for him?' (Psalm 8:3–4).

The witness of God's marvellous creation is there for anyone and everyone to observe. The stars that we can see in the clear night sky, and the many more that lie beyond our sight, are called a galaxy. It is estimated that there are one hundred billion stars in our galaxy and that there are one hundred million galaxies in the whole of known space. Some scientists go further and suggest that known space is one billionth part of what is possibly all space. With the naked eye, we can see between three and four thousand stars on a clear night. A small telescope will reveal almost two million, whereas a radio telescope will show us thousands of millions. It is estimated that there are thirty thousand million stars in the Milky Way alone—that great splash of tiny stars closely packed together in the night sky. Some suggest this figure should be ten to the power of eleven.[1] All such figures are bewildering.

The intricate complexity of even the simplest part of this creation, the panoramic beauty of a magnificent landscape, the kaleidoscope of colour, sight, sense and sound, should all tell us something about the wisdom, majesty and power of the God who made it all. It takes a far greater leap of faith to believe that all this design came about as the result of chance over billions of years, than to accept it as the creative plan of a wise designer, architect, engineer and craftsman. That, after all, is the very least that we assume when we are confronted with a beautifully laid out garden, a stunning building, a complex piece of machinery or an intricate tapestry.[2]

We are expected to agree with the prophet who, seven hundred years before the coming of Christ, wrote,

'Who has measured the waters in the hollow of his hand, or with the breadth of his hand marked off the heavens? Who has held the dust of the earth in a basket, or weighed the mountains on the scales and the hills in a balance? Who has understood the mind of the LORD, or instructed him as his counsellor? Whom did the LORD

---

1 David Baker in *Astronomy* (Hamlyn 1989 revised ed), p. 230 even doubles that figure.
2 For vivid details of the irreducible complexity of planet Earth and the universe revealing the hand of the Creator see Stuart Burgess and Andy McIntosh, *Wonders of Creation—Design in a fallen world* (Day One Publications, Leominster 2017).

consult to enlighten him, and who taught him the right way? Who was it that taught him knowledge or showed him the path of understanding?' (Isaiah 40:12–14).

No generation, tribe or nation has ever been left without a revelation of God. Speaking at Lystra nineteen hundred years ago, the apostle Paul insisted that, 'The living God, who made heaven and earth and sea and everything in them … has not left himself without testimony' (Acts 14:15–17). He presented this same truth when writing to the Christians at Rome:

'What may be known about God is plain to them, because God has made it plain to them. For since the creation of the world God's invisible qualities—his eternal power and divine nature—have been clearly seen, being understood from what has been made, so that men are without excuse.' (Romans 1:19–21).

Jesus emphasised the same point simply when he asserted, 'He causes his sun to rise on the evil and the good, and sends rain on the righteous and the unrighteous'(Matthew 5:45).

The awesome complexity and incredible beauty of creation has meant that no people group has ever been discovered that does not worship: they may bow down to sticks or stones, honour the sun or the moon, or live in fear of the spirits of the anaconda, antelope, or ancestors, but worship they must. It is inborn in the human race somehow to reach out after God in an attempt to find him (Acts 17:26–27).

However, despite this clear revelation by God of himself through nature, the spiritual blindness of everyone is apparently so great that no one will ever find God through creation alone. Ever since the entrance of sin and its results into the world, everything has been spoiled and the whole of creation is bound to a principle of death and decay (Romans 8:20–21). This is what we mean by 'nature red in tooth and claw'. For many, creation is no longer seen as an infallible guide to God because it does not always appear to reflect the purpose of a kind and loving Creator.

REVELATION IN THE MIND AND CONSCIENCE

In the Bible, King Solomon once tried hard not to believe in God. He shook off religion like a dog shaking the water from its hair. But this once wise king discovered that he could never get God and a belief in eternity out of his mind. The dog may shake itself dry, but the river is still there. Solomon was wise enough to know the reason for all this: '[God] has set eternity in the hearts of men' (Ecclesiastes 3:11). Men and women are made to worship God, but sin has so spoiled the human mind and soul that instead of worshipping the Creator, they worship the creature; they exchange the glory of God for an image of creation (Romans 1:23). Once again, it is not the revelation that is at fault.

In the same way, throughout the world and across every culture in all generations, people have a knowledge of right and wrong; what we referred to earlier as a moral consciousness. Cultures may not always agree *what* is right and wrong, but all agree that there *is* a right and wrong. Once again, in the New Testament Paul expressed this very clearly:

'When Gentiles, who do not have the law, do by nature things required by the law, they are a law for themselves, even though they do not have the law, since they show that the requirements of the law are written on their hearts, their consciences also bearing witness, and their thoughts now accusing, now even defending them' (Romans 2:14–15).

This knowledge of right and wrong is also part of God's revelation, but because of sin even this is unreliable. Paul referred to those whose 'consciences have been seared as with a hot iron (1 Timothy 4:2). To a degree this is true of everyone; from the playroom to the boardroom people learn to lie, and even at times believe their own lie. Some may have a more sensitive conscience than others, but for everyone, we have a conscience that is no longer wholly reliable. Throughout history, nations are led to accept the most appalling atrocities, societies adopt degrading life-styles and religions advocate cruel brutality simply because they are persuaded it is right. When the clear objective moral code from the Creator God is ignored, the human conscience runs wild.

Chapter 1

REVELATION IN PROVIDENCE AND HISTORY

The history of the world and its civilizations can only be understood properly in the light of God and his purpose for the church. In the Old Testament God revealed himself as the God of Israel, and the Jews came to know him as the 'God who brought you out' from Egypt (Exodus 6:7). The history of the Exodus was a revelation of God. In Acts 17:26–27 Paul declared to the philosophers of Athens that both history and geography belong to God:

'From one man, he made every nation of men, that they should inhabit the whole earth; and he determined the times set for them [history] and the exact places where they should live [geography]. God did this so that men would seek him and perhaps reach out for him and find him'

God's purpose in revealing himself in the providence of history is to lead the human race to himself.

Similarly, just as Jesus pointed to the kindness of God in allowing both the evil and the good, the righteous and the unrighteous, to enjoy his sun and rain (Matthew 5:45), so Paul reminded the citizens of Lystra: 'He has not left himself without testimony: He has shown kindness by giving you rain from heaven and crops in their seasons; he provides you with plenty of food and fills your hearts with joy' (Acts 14:17). God's good gifts of sun and rain, the seasons of the year, health and strength, beauty and love, are all part of God's revelation of himself.

Not everyone will have equal portions of God's general revelation. Some may see little of his providential love and care because of their desperate circumstances of famine or poverty, and others, through the loss of sight, may never see the beauty of creation. But the Bible makes it clear that everyone has sufficient evidence of God, even if it is only that voice of conscience that tells them there is a God.[3]

We cannot fully understand history unless we see in it God working out his purposes in this world. History belongs to God; it is his story.

---

3   In 1678, the Puritan John Flavel published *The Mystery of Providence*. With numerous examples he illustrated the evidence of God in all events of life. Available today from The Banner of Truth Trust.

However, because of the tragic results of sin, not all parts of history equally reflect the goodness and justice of God; so much reflects the cruelty and greed of the human race; even then, history belongs to God and is intended to teach us what happens when God is left out—although it is rarely understood as such.

Special revelation

APPEARANCES, DREAMS, VISIONS AND MIRACLES

During the Old Testament period, there were occasions when God appeared in a visible form to his people. This is called a 'theophany' and the word comes from a Greek noun meaning 'God' and a verb meaning 'to appear'. These 'appearings' are often spoken of as 'the angel of the LORD'. Hagar met with the Lord (Genesis 16:7–13) and so did Abraham just before the destruction of Sodom and Gomorrah (Genesis 18). Jacob met a stranger by the river Jabbok whom he identified as the Lord, and said, 'I saw God face to face' (Genesis 32:22–31). Joshua (Joshua 5:13–15), Gideon (Judges 6:11–24) and Manoah (Judges 13:2–23) had similar experiences, as did the three friends in the fiery furnace (Daniel 3:25). In a theophany, God the Father was revealing himself through his Son even before Christ's birth at Bethlehem.

Dreams and visions were also used by God to reveal himself and his plans. Jacob saw something of the Lord in his dream during that first restless night when he fled from his brother's revenge (Genesis 28:13). In the year of King Uzziah's death the prophet Isaiah went into the temple and there saw the glory of the Lord (Isaiah 6); from John 12:41 it is clear that this was Christ's glory. There are at least six accounts of God speaking through dreams and visions in the Acts of the Apostles, including Peter's vision in chapter 10. Even godless kings like Pharaoh, Nebuchadnezzar and Belshazzar received revelations of God's purposes either through dreams (Genesis 41:1, 25; Daniel 2:1), a direct voice from heaven (Daniel 4:31), or some other appearance (Daniel 5:5).

Miracles, in both the Old and New Testaments, had only one main purpose and that was to reveal something of the character of God. Moses was sent to Pharaoh to perform miracles, 'that you may know that I am the LORD' (Exodus 10:2), and Christ's first miracle was to 'reveal his glory' (John 2:11).

However, although the revelation was not at fault, such was the darkness of the human mind that many ignored or misunderstood the power and love of God in these revelations. Besides, they were limited in both scope and duration; not many experienced them, and not many benefited from them.

CHRIST AS THE WORD

The greatest example of God revealing himself in history is his incarnation in Jesus Christ. God had spoken of this right at the dawn of history in Genesis 3:15. He confirmed it to Abraham in Genesis 12:3 and according to Galatians 3:8 the promise was fulfilled in Christ. We can never understand history before the coming of Christ unless we see in it God preparing the world, and 'when the time had fully come, God sent his Son' (Galatians 4:4). See in this series Book 1 chapters 1 and 2 for the Master Plan and prophecy.)

John in his Gospel refers to Christ as 'the Word' (John 1:1). Because it is chiefly by words that we reveal ourselves to each other and communicate with each other, it is appropriate that God should use 'Word' as the title for his Son. The three disciples on the hilltop with Jesus saw him transformed into his heavenly glory and then heard the voice of God: 'This is my Son, whom I have chosen; listen to him' (Luke 9:35). God spoke not just through the words of Jesus in his teaching, but through his character.

Earlier we noted that David thought of creation having words, 'speaking' about God. However, when God wanted to reveal himself as fully as the rebellious human race could understand, he spoke through Christ. Christ is God's greatest Word to mankind—the fullest expression of the character of God that we could ever have on earth. He claimed: 'Anyone who has seen me has seen the Father' (John 14:9).

Writing to the Hebrew Christians, the apostle made the incredible claim that: 'In these last days [God] has spoken to us by his Son... The Son is the radiance of God's glory, and *the exact representation of his being...*' (Hebrews 1:2–3). This last phrase can be correctly translated from the original: 'He is the exact character of the actual reality of God himself.' However, although Jesus *perfectly* revealed the Father, he did not *fully* reveal him, because the awesome character of the Triune God was masked by the perfect humanity of Jesus. There is so much more of the full character of God that we will never grasp here. Yet, there can be no better or more precise visible revelation on earth of God than Jesus Christ.

But Christ is no longer visible to us, so how can we be sure of this greatest revelation?

SCRIPTURE AS THE WORD

The book that we call the Bible is God's collected verbal revelation. It does not contain all the words that he has even given, but all that he wants us to have. It contains all we need for our knowledge of God and his saving love. In God's general revelation we saw that the sin and spiritual blindness of the human race draws a curtain across our understanding. In countless ways, God reveals himself clearly and without error, and if men and women were not sinful then the beauty and design of creation would be sufficient to lead them to true worship. However, God has given something that is sufficient and—like all of his revelation—perfect and without error. He has given us the Bible. Without this, a fallen world would not know reliably about the Triune God and the need and way of salvation. Just as Jesus Christ is the fullest expression of the character of God on earth, so the Bible is the fullest expression of the will of God in this world.

However, the Bible does not tell us all there is to know, or even all that we want to know. Like a serial, the story will not be ended until God closes the final chapter. Each part of the Bible is a little more revelation.

The Bible is not just another way in which God gets his message across, nor is it merely the means by which we learn of salvation. The Bible is part of God's way of salvation itself. It is not merely a witness to God's revelation; it *is* God's revelation. It is God breaking through the barrier of sin and revealing himself and his salvation in the simplest and most sufficient way possible.

The Bible does not *contain* God's word; it *is* God's word. Nor does the Bible *become* God's word when it speaks to us; it is *always* God's word, whether we acknowledge this or not. The Bible is never dependent upon our response for its authority. The laws of a nation do not depend for their authority upon the obedience of every citizen; on the contrary, law carries the authority of the government regardless of our obedience. In the same way God, as the highest authority, has given us the Bible and it carries the fullest possible authority regardless of anyone's response. Similarly, the Bible does not only contain stories of God's love; it is in itself an expression of God's love.

In October 2002, BBC1 ran a series entitled 'The Pyramid'. It was the story of the great pyramid of King Kufu of Egypt, and it set out to answer the questions how and why it was built. The short series concluded with the following words: 'What happens when we die and what should that mean to us while we are alive? These are the greatest of all questions— and the Egyptian answer was the Great Pyramid.' These may well be the greatest of all questions asked by mankind, but the Christian answer lies in the Bible. Because of this the Bible must be a book beyond error. If it is not, then God's final and clearest revelation of himself, and his answers to the greatest of all questions, are less reliable than the stars in the sky or the Great Pyramid of King Kufu.

In every area of life, accurate communication is vital. Whether in the family or society, in the classroom or boardroom, on the sports field or battlefield, it is essential that those with instructions are able to communicate clearly and accurately so that the important information they have to pass on is not jumbled beyond recognition. Nowhere is this more important than when the Sovereign God communicates with sinful and rebellious humanity. We now turn to the subject of how carefully and accurately God has communicated his words to the entire human race.

2. Ultimate truth

What do we mean by 'inspired and without error'? Is this what the Bible claims, and has this always been the teaching of the Christian church?

To say that the Bible is the word of God and therefore without error because the Bible itself claims this, is seen by many as an argument in circles. It is like saying, 'This prisoner must be innocent because he says he is.' Are we justified in appealing to the Bible's own claim in settling this matter of its authority and inerrancy?

Self-authentication—the witness of the Bible to itself

OUR WORD SHOULD BE ENOUGH

This is known as 'Self-authentication', and it is used constantly in our daily experience. When someone writes their own life story, much of it can never be checked because it could not be known unless the author revealed it. They may write about their childhood fears or memories and we must take their word for this. We either believe what they say or distrust them. The same is true when someone relates a dream or tells us what they are thinking; no one can possibly confirm or deny the account since there is only one witness. In this case the reader or listener will rely entirely on self-authentication and will either believe it or not, depending upon how trustworthy the witness is known to be. This was exactly Paul's argument in 1 Corinthians 2:11 when he wrote, 'Who among men knows the thoughts of a man except the man's spirit within him? In the same way no one knows the thoughts of God except the Spirit of God.'

If people were not unreliable, witness to oneself would always be enough. In John 5:31–32 Jesus agreed with the principle that self-witness is normally not sufficient: 'If I testify about myself, my testimony is not valid. There is another who testifies in my favour, and I know that his testimony about me is valid.' Later, in John 8:13, the Pharisees took up this point when Jesus claimed, 'I am the light of the world.' They corrected him by saying, 'Here you are, appearing as your own witness; your testimony is not valid.' In defence Jesus showed that in his case, because he came from God the Father, self-witness is reliable: 'Even if I testify on my own behalf, my testimony is valid...' (v 14), and the verses that follow make clear his position that self-witness is reliable where sin does not interfere. Because Jesus was never found to be a false witness, and no one could prove him guilty of sin (John 8:46), his words could be trusted. In the same way, since the Bible is never found to be a false witness we have a right to listen to its own claim about itself.

Much of the Bible's history is such that unless God had revealed it we could never have known it. There are many scientific theories telling us how the world came into being. Some of these theories differ only slightly from each other, but others are contradictory. This only shows that no one can really be sure about such matters because no scientist was there when it all happened. Unless the God who was there has revealed it, we could never know for certain. The same is true for all the great Bible doctrines. How can we be sure of God's anger against sin, or his love for sinners, or his plans to choose a people for himself, unless God himself had told us?

THERE MUST BE A FINAL COURT OF APPEAL

When a person wants to confirm that what they are saying is true, they often appeal to someone or something greater than themselves; they swear on a holy book or say something like: 'God is my witness.' But God had no one greater than himself to confirm his word and therefore he appealed to his own character: 'When God made his promise to Abraham, since there was no one greater for him to swear by, he swore by himself...' (Hebrews 6:13). In law, there is always a final court of appeal, beyond which there is no higher authority. Therefore, if the Bible is God's word it must be its own witness. There can be no higher authority than God to witness to its truth. Hilary of Poitiers, a fourth century theologian, once claimed, 'Only God is a fit witness to himself.'

AUTHORITY IS TESTED BY ITS RESULTS

This was a principle Jesus recognised in John 10:37–38: 'Do not believe me unless I do what my Father does. But if I do it, even though you do not believe me, believe the miracles, that you may learn and understand that the Father is in me, and I in the Father.' This principle ran through the Old Testament also: 'You may say to yourselves, "How can we know when a message has not been spoken by the Lord?" If what a prophet proclaims in the name of the Lord does not take place or come true, that is a message the Lord has not spoken' (Deuteronomy 18:21–22).

If the Bible can be proved true wherever we can test it, then we are right to accept its word in those areas where we cannot test it. It is therefore essential that the Bible is seen to be accurate in its history, geography and prophecy—areas that we often can test—in order for us to trust its doctrine, which is an area we cannot test. If a prisoner on trial is found wholly trustworthy in matters that can be checked, he is more readily believed when he asserts things that cannot be checked. By contrast, if an author writing his autobiography is proved wrong on many of his supposed facts, then we are hardly willing to trust his word for those childhood memories either.

One value of the Bible embedded in, and recording, real history is that it can be checked. Book 5 chapters 2 and 3 of this series, will show that the historical accuracy of the biblical record is proven again and again.

THE BOOK THAT SPEAKS FOR ITSELF

During his lifetime, Jesus witnessed to the inspiration of the Old Testament, a subject we shall return to in the next chapter; and the Holy Spirit witnesses in the mind of the Christian. So often young Christians accept the authority of God's word without being told they must. It was through the Bible that they became a Christian and the same book speaks with a living power to their mind and heart each day. Of course, this does not prove that the Bible is true in every part, but this ring of truth is not insignificant. The church leaders in the first two or three centuries were confronted with other literature claiming to be written by apostles, and one way they had of clearly sifting out the false books was the authentic authority that was conveyed by the Scriptures. The Bible is a book that speaks for itself.

Two errors to be avoided

On 2 April 1792 William Pitt presented the House of Commons with a passionate speech against the slave trade, and among those in the House was William Wilberforce, who was the acknowledged leader of the crusade to end slavery. Wilberforce commented on that speech in his own diary and concluded, 'For the last twenty minutes he [Pitt] really seemed to be inspired.' Did Wilberforce, who himself believed in the total trustworthiness of the Bible, mean by that phrase that Pitt was speaking with inerrant accuracy? Of course not. He was using the word 'inspired' in a more general way, without any conscious reference to the infallible intervention of God.

In answering the question, 'What was God's method of inspiration?', we must be aware of two extremes.

GENERAL INSPIRATION

Admitting that the Bible is a very special book with a unique message, some claim that the writers were merely prompted by God to a deeper spiritual understanding than most men. But then, so the argument runs, the English poet Shakespeare and the French philosopher Voltaire were similarly 'inspired'—though perhaps not by God. Many of their ideas were good, but we must not say that their words were infallible. In a similar way, it is suggested that the Bible writers were spiritual and pious men but they were capable of error and at times were either too extreme, or too loose in their statements. It is suggested that we must bring our own reason and common sense to the Bible to remove the errors. Similarly, we talk of a friend having 'inspiration', when all we mean is that they had a good idea. Some people are described as 'an inspiration' simply because their life and work motives others to greater effort.

To use the word 'inspiration' in this way with reference to the Bible, ignores its own claim for itself as we will see. However, it also overlooks the fact that the way we convey the truth is through words. When we are learning a new language, we will often get our words wrong; we know exactly what we want to say, but we fail to communicate our message because we do not use the right words. If the words of the biblical writer are not exactly right, then however 'inspired' and well-meaning he may have been, we will never be sure of the true truth.

MECHANICAL (DICTATION) INSPIRATION

Another wrong view of 'inspiration' is that the human writers were little more than dictating machines or keyboards for a computer—they were not thinking, but simply wrote down letters and words as God dictated them. Admittedly such a view of the Bible would emphasize it as the word of God, but it is inaccurate for a number of reasons.

First, it ignores the obvious preparation of the writer by God. If God is merely dictating, the writer's only necessary qualification would be the ability to write neatly.

Second, it ignores the fact that the various writers in the Bible reveal their own character, style and culture, to such a degree that at times we can recognize characteristics of Paul's letters or John's Gospel in much the same way that people can recognize our own phrases and style from our letters and emails.

Third, it ignores the fact that some writers used the results of their own research into available documents. Long lists of family histories (genealogies) and official letters were almost certainly reproduced from government records. Some of the lists of names in Chronicles are 'records from ancient times' (1 Chronicles 4:22). See also, for example, 1 Kings 11:41; 1 Chronicles 29:29–30; Ezra 4:11–22 and Luke 1:1–4.

It is true that in the history of this debate over how the Bible came to us, some have referred to the Spirit 'dictating' what was written—John Calvin, John Wesley and many of the early church leaders, including Augustine, used this language. However, what they undoubtedly meant by this was that the Holy Spirit ensured the accuracy of the outcome, in much the same way that we might refer to an officer 'dictating' the deployment of his soldiers. Having said this, there is no reason why we should deny that some parts of Scripture were in fact dictated in the narrow sense of this word. The Ten Commandments were originally written by the finger of God (Deuteronomy 9:10).

The meaning of 'inspiration'

In the Bible, the phrase 'God-breathed' is found only in modern translations of 2 Timothy 3:16, 'All Scripture is God-breathed'. It is just one word in the Greek and in older versions was generally translated by 'inspired'. Usually this is explained as the divine 'inbreathing' into a man by God's Holy Spirit, with the result that the man speaks, or writes, with a quality, insight, accuracy and authority that are possible in no other form of human speaking or writing. The word *may* be defined as 'inbreathing', but it ought not to be!

The word 'inspire' came into our English language from the Latin *inspirare* via the Norman French *inspirer* and it was not used to refer to the Scriptures until the Reformation in the sixteenth century. William Tyndale, normally a most accurate translator, used the word 'inspire' in his 1526 English New Testament. The Greek word is *theopneustos*, and it is made up from two Greek words: *theos* ('God') and *pneuma* ('breath' or 'wind'). Our word 'theology' comes from the Greek word for 'God'; theology is the study of God. And our words 'pneumonia' and 'pneumatic' are derived from the Greek *pneuma*; they refer to breath or air.

Benjamin B Warfield was a brilliant biblical scholar and Professor of Theology at Princeton, New Jersey from 1887 until his death in 1921. He meticulously studied this word *theopneustos* in all its uses outside the Bible. He showed that it is always used in a passive sense, something that is breathed out, and never in an active sense, breathing into something.[4] Therefore, the word *theopneustos* does not mean 'breathed *into* by God' but more exactly 'breathed *out* by God'. There is a big difference between breathing into something and breathing out—inspiring and expiring!

---

4   Benjamin B Warfield (1851–1921), *The Inspiration and Authority of the Bible* (Presbyterian and Reformed Publishing Company, Philadelphia 1948), pp. 132–133.

This means that in 2 Timothy 3:16 there is no direct reference to the human writer at all. It is 2 Peter 1:20–21 that tells us about the human writer, and we shall look at that later. In 2 Timothy 3:16 there is no reference to the *method* by which we received the Scripture, but only to its *origin* (author), where it came from. It is not breathed into man, but breathed out by God. That is an important claim. The emphasis is on where the words came from (they were breathed out by God) and not on what happened to the human writer (God breathing into him his words).

If someone asks me: 'How did you get that new car I see on your drive?' I may reply, 'It was sold to me by a friend of mine.' Or I may say, 'I drove it home from my friend's house.' Both answers are correct, but the first tells me where the car came from—you notice the passive use of the verb: '*It was sold* to me.' On the other hand, the second answer tells me how the car came to be on my drive: '*I drove it* home'—and that is an active use of the verb. *Theopneustos* is passive, it tells us where the words came from.

The word 'inspiration' is therefore misleading and not strictly scriptural. However, it has become a technical term and we shall have to continue to use it, though with the correct understanding. 'God-breathed' is an excellent translation of the word *theopneustos*.

HOW MUCH OF THE BIBLE IS INSPIRED?

If 'inspired' really means 'God-breathed', then the claim of the Bible is that all Scripture, being God-breathed, is accurate, without error and can therefore be trusted completely. God would cease to be God if he breathed out errors and contradictions, even in the smallest part. So long as we give *theopneustos* its true meaning, we shall not find it hard to understand the inerrancy of the Bible.

However, some do find it hard to accept this. Many have a more liberal view of Scripture and they cannot accept the supernatural, such as miracles, nor will they trust the words of Moses, Paul, or even Jesus himself. Others accept the words of Jesus but believe that Paul, John and Peter were not always correct. Still others believe that the doctrines revealed in the Bible are reliable and so are most, but not all, of the historical facts. As we saw earlier, a significant error is to conclude that the Bible only becomes the word of God when it speaks to the individual. To various extents each of these views denies the true meaning of *theopneustos*.

A few more cautions are needed to be sure that we do not misunderstand what we mean by 'inspiration'

THE ORIGINAL WRITER

When we refer to 'inspiration' we are referring to the original writers of Scripture, whether it was Moses, Isaiah, Paul or John etc. Unfortunately, we do not have any of the original 'autographs', as they are called, but only copies. This subject will be examined in detail in Book 4 chapters 2 to 4 of this series, but it is sufficient here to emphasise that in the many copies of copies that have been made over the centuries, small errors of transcription have crept into the text. However, these are small, rare and often understandable. One small stroke of the pen, for example, can alter a Hebrew number; one letter omitted can alter a Greek word. Nothing of importance, and certainly no doctrine or teaching, is affected by these small copyist's errors. Besides, the New Testament writers, and Jesus himself, were using copies—and a Greek translation of the Hebrew Scriptures—and they had total confidence in their authority and accuracy.

THE WORDS OF MEN

Whilst the whole of Scripture is God's word in the sense that it is part of his revelation, not everything is a word from God. Included in the Bible are the words of men and women, some of them pagan and evil people; and even the words of the devil himself, as we find in the account of the very first temptation and in the book of Job. There are even lies in the Bible! Here is one example: When God sent a young prophet to King Jeroboam he ordered the prophet to deliver his message and return home at once without accepting any hospitality. On the way, he met an old prophet who, wanting to entertain the younger man, claimed, 'I too am a prophet, as you are. And an angel said to me by the word of the LORD: "Bring him back with you to your house so that he may eat bread and drink water"' (1 Kings 13:18). Unfortunately he was lying, and the Scripture says so. When we speak of the Bible as without error, we mean that even these words are an accurate record of what the old prophet spoke.

We must also allow that at times we have the record of the personal views of that writer, which may not always be in harmony with truth. In the book of Job, for example, it is evident from God's assessment of Job's three friends that much of their professed 'wisdom' was, in fact, misguided and wrong (Job 42:7–9). Inerrancy means that this is exactly how they felt and what they said; it is the role of exegesis (explaining the words and context) and hermeneutics (understanding the meaning) to discover when we are hearing a timeless truth.

OFFICIAL RECORDS

It is evident that some writers used available documents from carefully stored archives. We are not to suppose that Moses or Nehemiah reproduced lists of genealogies from their memory, least of all their imagination. Verbal inerrancy does not demand that all details were corrected if, here or there, there was an error in the list; it simply guarantees that this is an accurate record of the document. There is a caution to be added to this concession and we will return to it in Book 5 chapter 4 'Guidelines for combat' in this series.

PLENARY AND VERBAL INSPIRATION

There are two words that are sometimes used to explain what evangelicals really mean when they speak about the Bible as God's word: plenary and verbal inspiration. 'Plenary' comes from the Latin *plenus*, which means 'full', and refers to the fact that the whole of Scripture *in every part* is God-given. 'Verbal' comes from the Latin *verbum* which means 'word' and emphasizes that even *the words* of Scripture are God-given. By definition, plenary and verbal inspiration means that the Bible is God-given (and therefore without error) in every part (doctrine, history, geography, dates, names) and in every single word.

Today, some use these words 'plenary' and 'verbal' yet mean something different. They say there are errors in the Bible, just small ones here and there, but these need not be counted against plenary and verbal inspiration because the facts that the Bible intended to state are what matters. One writer has expressed it like this: 'The implicit claim of biblical narrative is to be reasonably accurate.'[5] Notice, only '*reasonably* accurate'.

This is a variation on the view that we should distinguish between infallibility and inerrancy. Some claim that the message is infallible even though the words may be in error. It is suggested that we need only trouble ourselves to discover what the Bible *intends* to say, and if some details are incorrect, no matter. However, although there is a proper use of discovering what the Bible intends to say, to use 'intention' to cover up possible errors is incorrect. It is like a football team discounting all goals scored against it by the argument that it was never its intention to let the ball into the net. Such reasoning may satisfy its supporters, but certainly not its opponents! A witness to a crime may give a lot of details to the court, but if many of them are proved to be false, the witness cannot be allowed to plead, 'Well, what I intended to say was that I saw the crime, and in that everyone agrees I am right.' The fact is that he has lied, or at best has proved himself an unreliable witness, and no court will take him seriously.

The writer quoted above criticises the view of full inerrancy since, he claims, 'it is not directly asserted by Christ or within Scripture itself'.[6] He believes it is therefore a deduction from Scripture rather than plainly taught in Scripture, and he suggests that it is better to work from the observable facts (he calls it the 'phenomena') of Scripture. In other words, the argument runs like this: there clearly *are* errors and contradictions in the Bible, so we should discover a doctrine of inspiration that fits with that fact. There are two responses to this approach.

---

5   John Goldingay, *Models for Scripture* (Clements Publishing, Toronto 2004), p. 282. The author here claims, 'Material that is unhistorical is not uninspired. The whole text is God's inspired word. If certain points in Luke are unhistorical, those parts of this inspired Gospel also contribute to an inspired portrait of Jesus that can be effective and meaningful for its hearers.' This is a too-common misunderstanding of the meaning and importance of inerrancy, and makes little sense to most readers.

6   As above, p. 273.

First, there are other doctrines that are deduced from Scripture rather than are plainly stated. The most obvious being the doctrine of the Trinity, which is never spelt out in the Bible by the use of the word 'Trinity'. That doctrine is understood from the fact that the Father, Son and Holy Spirit are each equally revealed as truly and fully God.

A second response is that to arrive at a doctrine of inspiration based on the 'phenomena' of Scripture (ie we can allow some errors and contradictions because there clearly are errors and contradictions) fails to acknowledge that the 'errors and contradictions' have been shown to be more apparent than real.

We should never look at the problems and then work towards a doctrine; rather we should discover the doctrine from the Bible and then resolve the problems. That is a very important principle to cover many other areas of theology and biblical interpretation also—not least the early chapters of Genesis.

We must be alert to any understanding of 'inspiration' that limits the full inerrancy of the Scriptures.

Why is inerrancy important?

Those who believe in biblical inerrancy are sometimes accused of spending too much of their time 'straining at a gnat' whilst the big issue should be what the Bible teaches. This is both untrue and unfair. No group of Christians has been more exact in their interest in what the whole Bible says and in comparing Scripture with Scripture to discover the word of God, and no preachers have been more precise in biblical exposition, than those who affirm inerrancy. Besides, the subject is only dealt with because it is denied. To ignore it would lay them open to the charge of avoiding any challenge to their faith.

Is this whole debate about whether or not the Bible contains nothing but the truth merely a theological quibble? Certainly not. The question of ultimate authority is of the highest importance for the Christian, and for many reasons.

INERRANCY GOVERNS OUR ATTITUDE TO THE TRUTH OF THE GOSPEL

We cannot offer the world a reliable gospel presented in an unreliable Scripture. How can we be sure of truth on any issue if we are suspicious of errors anywhere? An airline pilot will ground his aircraft even on suspicion of the most minor of faults, because he is aware that one fault destroys confidence in the complete machine. If the history contained in the Bible is wrong how can we be sure that the doctrine or moral teaching is correct? Some theologians claim that it is the real message of the biblical writer that is important and that if the writer is incorrect in several facts, or even makes them up, it does not at all alter the truth of his message. But in no other area of life would we accept this argument.

A farmer, wishing to sell an animal to a neighbour, may describe in great detail its size and weight, food intake and milk and butterfat output, its age and characteristics, and then add that it is a light brown Jersey cow. If, on the following day, he arrives with a black and white Holstein Friesian, his neighbour will quite rightly distrust all the important details given the previous day. Either it is a different cow or the farmer does not know his animals. When I collected my car from a service on one occasion, I noticed that although the list of items to be checked included refilling the windscreen wash bottle, the mechanic clearly had not done so. The foreman suggested it was a very small item, but I pointed out that if they missed something so obvious and simple, I had good reason to question what else of greater importance they might have overlooked.

These are not theoretical objections. Some who claim to hold a high view of the inspiration of Scripture have nevertheless suggested that parts of the Gospel stories have been influenced by Jewish tradition or prophecies in the Hebrew Scriptures. Thus a few unhistorical elements in the narrative of Jesus' birth and Luke's account of Judas' death in Acts 1:18–19 are perfectly acceptable. It is a short step from this to allowing that Paul may have been mistaken in some of his statements also—perhaps, for example, his claim in 1 Corinthians 15:6 that five hundred saw the risen Christ? When writers assert that 'Factual error need not hinder effectiveness and meaningfulness' and that the 'narrative parts make no claim to be dictated by God', they limit the 'all Scripture' of 2 Timothy 3:16. Should someone provide us with a list of what we can and cannot accept as historical fact? Is it no longer necessary to look for an explanation to an apparent contradiction or historical glitch in the Bible? Do we simply assume an error and move on with a shrug?

The heart of the Christian message is rooted in history. The incarnation (God becoming a man) is proved by the virgin birth of Jesus Christ. Redemption (the price being paid for man's rebellion to be forgiven) is obtained by his death on the cross. Reconciliation (the privilege of the sinner becoming a friend of God) is gained through the resurrection and ascension of Christ. If the recorded events are not true, how do we know that the theology behind them is true?

INERRANCY GOVERNS OUR ATTITUDE TO THE VALUE OF JESUS CHRIST

We cannot have a reliable Saviour without a reliable Scripture. If, as some suggest, the stories in the Gospels are not historically true and the recorded words of Jesus are occasionally inaccurate, how do we know what we can trust about who Jesus was and what he came to do? Must we rely upon the conflicting interpretations of a host of critical scholars before we know what Jesus Christ was like, or what he said? Or, if the Gospel stories are merely the result of the wishful thinking of the church in the second century, or even the personal views of the Gospel writers, then our faith no longer rests upon the historical Jesus but upon the opinions of men. Who will want to trust an unreliable Saviour for their eternal salvation?

To doubt the virgin conception and the literal resurrection of Jesus has significant implications for his character and purpose. The first underlines his perfect human nature and the second his power over death. If the Gospels, which are plain and straightforward on these two points, are wrong, then we must despair of ever understanding what it means about anything. Or, as Paul writes, 'Our preaching is useless… we are found to be false witnesses… your faith is futile, you are still in your sins [and] those who have fallen asleep in Christ are lost… we are to be pitied more than all men' (1 Corinthians 15:14–19). Not a little hangs on the historical reality of the resurrection.

However, to accept the big issues like the virgin conception and the resurrection, and yet admit small errors elsewhere, leaves open the questions: What is a 'small' error and when is it significant? The problems raised by those who claim a 'high view of Scripture' but deny inerrancy are far greater than those caused by upholding it.

INERRANCY GOVERNS OUR INTERPRETATION OF SCRIPTURE

The issue of the Bible and science is not our subject here. However, if we believe the Bible contains errors, then we can readily accept scientific theories that appear to prove the Bible wrong. We will allow the conclusions of science, contemporary views of geology for example, to govern our understanding of the Bible, even though the history of scientific theories is full of spectacular reverses of opinion; claims by 'experts' in one field or another have often proved lamentably short-sighted and disastrously wrong.

When we doubt inerrancy, we have to invent new principles for interpreting Scripture that for convenience turn history into poetry and facts into myths. It means that the first question a person must answer when they turn to a passage of the Bible is this, 'How reliable is this passage?' Only then will they be able to decide what to make of it. See Book 6 chapters 2 and 3 in this series on how to understand the Bible.

On the other hand, a belief in inerrancy means that we will test those theories by Scripture. A Bible in error is at the mercy of the wisdom of the current opinions of science, but an inerrant Bible submits to no man's judgement.

Scriptural inerrancy is a higher principle than scientific theories, and this means that we will be prepared to accept those passages that are written as history but which may seem to be contradicted by some scientific views. The account of creation, Jonah and his submarine experience, the miracles in the Bible, the virgin conception of Jesus Christ and his resurrection are all examples of plain historical writing that conflict with the views of unbelieving science.

INERRANCY GOVERNS OUR ATTITUDE TO THE PREACHING OF SCRIPTURE

A denial of biblical inerrancy always leads to a loss of confidence in Scripture both in the pulpit and in the pew. It was not the growth of education and science that emptied churches, nor two world wars, but the cold deadness of theological liberalism. See Book 5 chapter 1 in this series for a short history of biblical criticism. If the Bible's history is doubtful and its words are open to dispute, then people understandably lose confidence in it. Must every preacher first check with the latest view of critical scholarship before he can claim any authority for a passage from the Bible? If he has to discover whether a particular verse is what Jesus actually said, or what Matthew thought Jesus said, or what the second century church wanted Matthew to say that Jesus said, then he is not likely to have much confidence in what he himself eventually says.

Besides, most congregations have better things to do than listen to this. People want authority. They want to know what God has said. Where inerrancy is denied there is no longer clear authority. A church without authority is like a crocodile without teeth; it can open its mouth as wide and as often as it likes, but who cares?

At one time, doctrinal statements used the word 'infallible' to describe the Bible. That is a good word, though unfortunately it became less and less usable as some theologians employed it but denied that the Bible was without error. This is a false distinction, because you cannot have infallibility without inerrancy, though you can have inerrancy without infallibility. I may make a statement that in every respect is wholly factual and without error, but that does not make me infallible; however, if I am infallible then all my statements will be without error. Only God is infallible, and if the Bible is his revelation then it is inerrant because he is infallible.

INERRANCY PROTECTS THE CHARACTER OF GOD

Almost all theologians agree that Scripture is in some measure God's revelation to the human race. But to allow that it contains error implies that God has mishandled inspiration and has allowed his people to be deceived for centuries until the twentieth century scholars began to disentangle the confusion. The alternative is that God has revealed himself plainly and without error in words that carry his eternal authority, and by their trustworthiness reflect his honour and character. Origen of Alexandria, in the third century, claimed: 'If we believe for certain that the Gospels were written with the cooperation of the Holy Spirit, those who wrote them could not have had any lapse of memory.'[7]

Does the Bible claim to be God-breathed and without error?

Some of the strongest critics of the Bible, who themselves deny inerrancy, have admitted that this was clearly the belief of Jesus and the apostles. The German theologians Adolf Harnack (1851–1930) and Rudolf Bultmann (1884–1976) are examples of this. F C Grant, of Union Seminary in the United States of America, a very liberal critic of the Bible, has written of the New Testament: 'Everywhere it is taken for granted that what is written in Scripture is the work of divine inspiration and is therefore trustworthy, infallible, and inerrant.' He then added: 'What is described or related in the Old Testament is unquestionably true.'[8]

We will look at the biblical position briefly here and return to it in the following chapters.

THE VIEW OF THE OLD TESTAMENT WRITERS

The Old Testament writers saw their message as God-breathed and therefore wholly reliable.

God confirmed this to Moses and future prophets in Deuteronomy 18:18: 'I will raise up for them a prophet like you from among their brothers; I will put my words in his mouth, and he will tell them everything I command him.' This was also Jeremiah's experience at the beginning of his ministry: 'Then the Lord reached out his hand and touched my mouth and said to me, "Now, I have put my words in your mouth"' (Jeremiah 1:9).

The Hebrew word for prophet means 'a spokesman' and the prophet's message was: 'This is what the Sovereign Lord says'—an expression

---

7 Origen, *Commentary on Matthew*, XVI.12.
8 Frederick C Gran, *An Introduction to New Testament Thought* (Abingdon Press, New York 1950), p. 75.

that, in one form or another, occurs over five hundred times in the Old Testament. As a result, they frequently so identified themselves with God that they spoke as though God himself was actually speaking. Isaiah 5 reveals this clearly. In verses 1–2 the prophet speaks of God in the third person *(he)* then in verses 3–6 there is a change, and Isaiah speaks in the first person *(I)*. Isaiah has become the actual voice of God. It is little wonder that King David could speak of the word of the Lord as 'flawless' (2 Samuel 22:31 and see also Proverbs 30:5).

THE NEW TESTAMENT AGREES WITH THE OLD

Peter and John saw the words of David in Psalm 2 not as the opinion of a king of Israel, but as the voice of God. They introduced a quotation from that psalm in a prayer to God: 'You spoke by the Holy Spirit through the mouth of your servant, our father David' (Acts 4:25). Similarly, Paul accepted Isaiah's words as God himself speaking to men: 'The Holy Spirit spoke the truth to your forefathers when he said through Isaiah the prophet…' (Acts 28:25).

So convinced were the writers of the New Testament that all the words of the Old Testament Scripture were the actual words of God that they even claimed, 'Scripture says,' when the words quoted came directly from God. Two examples are Romans 9:17: 'For the Scripture says to Pharaoh,' and Galatians 3:8: 'The Scripture … announced the gospel in advance to Abraham…' In Hebrews 1 many of the Old Testament passages quoted were originally addressed to God by the psalmist, yet the writer to the Hebrews refers to them as the words of God.

Jesus believed in verbal inspiration

Clearly Jesus believed that the words of the Old Testament were God-breathed. Here are three examples:

- In John 10:34 (quoting from Psalm 82:6) Jesus based his teaching upon a phrase: 'I said, "You are gods."'

- In Matthew 22:32 Jesus emphasised the words, 'I am', in Exodus 3:6. He was in conflict with the Sadducees who denied the resurrection of the body. If God had said to Moses, 'I *was* the God of Abraham,

Isaac and Jacob,' or even if he had meant, 'I am the God who was worshipped by Abraham, Isaac and Jacob,' then Jesus had established nothing by quoting this verse from Exodus. In fact, the present tense 'I am' is all important and forms the basis of his argument. In its Old Testament context, the verb is understood as God saying to Moses: 'I am still the God of Abraham, Isaac and Jacob. I am not the God of dead men, but living men; their death has been conquered and their resurrection is certain.' We should note here as a matter of accuracy that the Hebrew of Exodus 3:6 does not contain a verb, only the personal pronoun 'I'. However, in such a case the present tense is understood. The *Septuagint*—the Greek translation of the Old Testament (see chapter 4 here)—does contain the present tense of the verb and Jesus used the present tense in Matthew 22:32. In all this, he settled the issue of God's eternal existence by reference to one word in the Hebrew Old Testament.

• In Matthew 22:43–44 Jesus quoted from Psalm 110:1 and emphasized a single word, 'Lord'. Here he was revealing himself as the Son of God.

PAUL BELIEVED IN VERBAL INSPIRATION

In a significant passage, Paul based an argument upon the fact that a particular word in the Old Testament is singular and not plural. Writing to the Galatians, Paul claimed that in God's promises to Abraham God does not say, '"and to seeds", meaning many people, but "and to your seed", meaning one person, who is Christ' (Galatians 3:16). Paul was quoting from Genesis 12:7; 13:15; 22:18 and 24:7. In each verse our translators use the word 'offspring' and the Hebrew word is in the singular. Paul's argument here is that God's chief purpose is not to refer to Israel as the offspring of Abraham, but to Christ.

It may rightly be argued that the singular of this particular word can also have a plural meaning—in English also the word 'offspring' can refer to one or many; it is also true that in Galatians 3:29 Paul used the word (in this case 'seed' instead of 'offspring') with the plural meaning. What is significant, however, is the way Paul drew attention to the fact that the Hebrew word in Genesis is singular when God could have chosen a plural word. As far as Paul is concerned God chose the singular for a special purpose because it emphasized that the greatest descendant of Abraham was Christ (singular) and that by faith in him many become spiritual descendants. This is a belief in verbal inspiration; it mattered to Paul whether God used a singular or plural in these passages of the Old Testament. It is therefore not surprising that in Romans 3:2 Paul gives as one advantage of being a Jew the fact that 'They have been entrusted with the very words of God.'

The method of inspiration

We have already seen that 2 Timothy 3:16 should be translated accurately: 'All Scripture is God-breathed.' This verse tells us of the origin of Scripture. It comes from God and its accuracy and authority are therefore plenary, covering every part, and verbal, covering even the words themselves. But there is one more question we must ask: 'How was the Bible inspired?'

2 Peter 1:20–21 will help us answer this question: 'No prophecy of Scripture came about by the prophet's own interpretation. For prophecy never had its origin in the will of man, but men spoke from God as they were carried along by the Holy Spirit.'

THE SCRIPTURES CAME THROUGH MEN

The claim of the Bible's critics is that since it was men who wrote down the words of Scripture, the light from heaven was broken up and spoilt by human error. To illustrate how the words of God are marred by man, reference is sometimes made to the pure rays of the sun broken and shaded as they filter through the trees of a thick forest, or the clear sunlight becoming a kaleidoscope of broken colour through a stained-glass window. However, we may use the same illustration with an opposite purpose. Suppose the Creator so designed the leaves and the trees that the light and shade falling across the forest floor are exactly what he intended? Or suppose the craftsman planned the window exactly as he wanted the colours to be reflected?

The Scriptures came from the pen of men prepared by God. God did not choose Paul as the most suitable man, he formed and equipped Paul for his sovereign purpose. If a commanding officer has an important message to relay to his troops, he will take every precaution to make sure the exact message he wants to communicate gets through. Armies spend time and money to ensure their communications network is of the highest possible standard of accuracy. It is possible today for a soldier to gain a satellite bearing on his location to within a few feet of accuracy; the expense of time and technology for that information was colossal. But God has something far more important to say to us, and his accuracy is greater than that of any man-made system.

In Galatians 1:11–24 Paul recounts his personal testimony. Among his claims are two of great importance: First, 'The gospel I preached is not something that man made up. I did not receive it from any man, nor was I taught it; rather, I received it by revelation from Jesus Christ' (vs 11–12). Second, 'God set me apart from birth and called me by his grace' (v 15). This was exactly the experience of the prophets Isaiah (49:1–2,5) and Jeremiah (1:5); and this is what Peter was referring to in 2 Peter 1:20–21 when he claimed, 'No prophecy of Scripture came about by the prophet's own interpretation.'

BUT NOT MEN LEFT TO THEMSELVES

It is wrong to think of the human writers of the Bible as co-authors with God. Certainly they reflected their own personality and employed their own style of writing, but they had nothing at all to do with the *origin* of the message; that belonged to God alone. However, although they wrote the God-breathed message in God's words, they were personally involved in the message. An officer may send a warning to the platoon of some danger that threatens it. The messenger is given a carefully prepared message which he delivers faithfully and exactly. The message is not his own, but the urgency of his voice and the excitement of his gestures are his own. The message has become part of his thinking and action. He feels the urgency, and although everyone knows that he is passing on the very words of the commanding officer, the soldiers can rightly claim, 'That man's message is very important.'

It is the same with the human writers of the Bible. The ultimate origin is not from themselves, they received it from God. It was not written for them on a sheet of paper like our military messenger, but in their minds, and it became so much a part of their thinking that it was their own message. They spoke it or wrote it with all the force and enthusiasm they could. It was exactly God's message, given by men. Peter assures us that the human writers were not free simply to interpret the message God gave to them. No officer allows his vital communication with the front-line troops to be interpreted by the soldier into a message he thinks the forces will best understand—or enjoy!

Three times in the Bible this relationship between the human messenger and the God-breathed message is spoken of as the writer 'eating' the words of God. One of these is in Jeremiah 15:16: 'When your words came, I ate them; they were my joy and my heart's delight.' The other two are in Ezekiel 2:8 to 3:3 and Revelation 10:8–11. As a result, the prophets often preached a message they did not fully understand; they preached God's words, not their own. This is Peter's claim in 1 Peter 1:10–12. In contrast to all this, false prophets were described as those 'who prophesy out of their own imagination' (Ezekiel 13:2). No commanding officer wants a messenger like that!

MEN 'MOVED' BY THE HOLY SPIRIT

The Greek word used here in 2 Peter 1:21 is *phero*, which means 'to bear' or 'to carry'. It was a familiar word to the sailor, referring to the ship carried along by the wind; and Peter used to be a fisherman on the Sea of Galilee. The human writers of the Bible certainly used their minds, but not to make up the message. The Holy Spirit carried them along in their thinking so that only his God-breathed words were recorded. The apostle Paul explained this in 1 Corinthians 2:13: 'This is what we speak, not in words taught us by human wisdom but in words taught by the Spirit.'

A summary therefore, is that 2 Timothy 3:16 tells us where the Scriptures came from, that is the origin of the Bible: it came *from God*.

2 Peter 1:20–21, on the other hand, tells us how the Scriptures came to us, that is the method by which we got our Bible: it came *through men*. This same distinction is seen also in the Old Testament. In Nehemiah 8:1 we read of 'the Book of the Law of Moses' and immediately we are informed, 'which the LORD had commanded for Israel'. This is the same as Peter's 'Men spoke from God'. Paul was similarly convinced when he wrote, 'Christ is speaking through me' (2 Corinthians 13:3).

WHAT DO WE MEAN BY 'INSPIRATION'?

With all this as a background, it is time to offer a definition of what we mean when we talk of the Bible as inspired by God.

> The Holy Spirit moved men to write. He allowed them to use their own style, culture, gifts and character, to use the results of their own study and research, to write of their own experiences and to express what was in their mind. At the same time, the Holy Spirit did not allow error to influence their writings; he overruled in the expression of thought and in the choice of words. Therefore, they recorded accurately all that God wanted them to say and exactly how he wanted them to say it, in their own character, style and language.

> The inspiration of Scripture is a harmony of the active mind of the writer and the sovereign direction of the Holy Spirit to produce God's inerrant and infallible word for the human race.

Who believes in 'inerrancy'?

Today a lot of printer's ink is spent on the question of whether or not the evangelical view of Scripture outlined here, represents the mainstream of Christian thought throughout the history of the church. Whilst most evangelicals are convinced that it does, some claim that inerrancy was never asserted until the late nineteenth and early twentieth centuries when it was given its clearest statement by B B Warfield. But is this true?

THE FIRST FIVE HUNDRED YEARS

Clement of Rome, writing to the church at Corinth in the first century, reminded them: 'Look carefully into the Scriptures, which are the true utterances of the Holy Spirit. Observe that nothing of an unjust or counterfeit character is written in them.'[9] In a similar way, late in the second century Justin Martyr wrote to a Jew he was seeking to win for Christ. In his *Dialogue with Trypho*, he claimed, 'I am entirely convinced that no Scripture contradicts another.'[10]

Tertullian led the church in Carthage, North Africa, in the second century and argued that whatever the Scripture teaches is true and binding upon us, and Clement of Alexandria called it the first principle of instruction because in it we hear the voice of the Lord. Irenaeus represented the Greek church in the second century and wrote a massive five volumes against the heresies of his day. In defending the absolute accuracy of the Scriptures he wrote, 'being most properly assured that the Scriptures are indeed perfect, since they were spoken by the Word of God and His Spirit.'[11] Expressing his confidence in Luke as a historian, Irenaeus continued, 'No person of common sense can permit them to receive some things recounted by Luke as being true, and to set others aside as if he had not known the truth.'[12]

We have already seen that Origen of Alexandria and Caesarea in the early part of the third century agreed with this: 'If we believe for certain that the Gospels were written with the cooperation of the Holy Spirit, those who wrote them could not have had any lapse of memory.'[13]

John Chrysostom, the 'golden-mouthed' preacher from Antioch in the fourth century, declared that even the most trivial statement in the Bible has more than superficial value since it all came from God; to those who held little value for the lists of names in the Bible he asserted, 'Note the force of the addition of one single syllable, and stop despising whole

9   *The First Epistle of Clement to the Corinthians*, 45.
10 Justin Martyr, *Dialogue with Trypho*, chapter 65.
11 Irenaeus, *Against Heresies*, 2.28.2.
12 Irenaeus, *Against Heresies*, 3.14.4.
13 Origen, *Commentary on Matthew*, 16:12.

names.'[14] One authority on John Chrysostom claims, 'Chrysostom understood very well that, because of Divine inspiration, it is impossible for the Holy Scriptures to contain errors.'[15]

In the same way Athanasius, the fourth century champion for the truth, recorded, 'The Sacred and divinely inspired Scriptures are sufficient for the exposition of the truth.'[16] He spoke also of 'the plain authority of the Scriptures' and 'the divine Scriptures'.

Augustine, possibly the greatest defender of the faith in the fifth century, represented the western church and claimed that the Bible books are 'free from error'.[17] Whilst he acknowledged some difficult places in Scripture, he allowed 'variations but not contradictions, diversities but not contrarieties.' On the biblical books, Augustine wrote to a friend: 'I have learned to yield such respect and honour only to the canonical books of Scripture. Of these do I most firmly believe that the authors were completely free from error.' He then added a wise qualification: 'And if in these writings I am perplexed by anything which appears to me opposed to truth, I do not hesitate to suppose that either the manuscript is faulty, or the translator has not caught the meaning of what was said, or I myself have failed to understand it.'[18] Elsewhere, writing to correct Jerome's poor understanding of Scripture, Augustine was equally clear: 'It seems to me that the most disastrous consequences must follow upon our believing that anything false is found in the sacred books...If you once admit into such a high sanctuary of authority one false statement... there will not be left a single sentence of these books which... may not be explained away.'[19]

---

14 Chrysostom, *Vigilae Christianae*, 22.
15 Chrysostomus Baur, *John Chrysostom and His Time* (Newman Press, Maryland 1959), Vol. 1, pp. 318–319.
16 Athanasius, *Against the Heathen*, 1.3.
17 John D Woodbridge, *Biblical Authority—a critique of the Rogers/McKim proposal* (Zondervan, Grand Rapids 1982), offers a detailed defence of Augustine's view of the Scriptures that cannot err, pp. 37–45.
18 Augustine, *Letters of Augustine*, 82.3.
19 Augustine, *Letters of Augustine*, 28.3.

If anything, the conclusion must be that the early church leaders, in their desire to lay full emphasis upon the divine inspiration and infallibility of the Scriptures, fell into the danger of overlooking the importance of the human authors and of leaning at times to a dictation view of inspiration. If they do not always use the word 'inerrancy' or the phrase 'without error', it is because those terms were not employed then. The above are representative of many more of the early church leaders who had no doubt as to the absolute inerrancy of Scripture. In the first five centuries at least, for Jews and Christians alike, if the Scriptures were the word of God they must be true and free from error.

THE REFORMATION AND BEYOND

The early Reformers, John Wycliffe (the 'morning star of the Reformation') and William Tyndale (our greatest English Bible translator), provide no support for anything other than a robust commitment to the absolute authority of Scripture. They both dedicated their lives wholly to the translation of the Bible into an English that the common people could understand. They did not use the phrase 'inerrancy', simply because the word had not been invented. However, their constant reference to the Bible as our final and supreme authority, and the absence of a discussion regarding its detailed accuracy, speaks clearly of their understood position at a time when it was not the detailed accuracy but the ultimate authority of the Bible that sent men and women to burn at the stake.

Despite claims to the contrary,[20] there can be little reasonable doubt that the Reformers in the sixteenth century not only followed the position of the early church leaders, but were in line with the understanding of the orthodox Protestant theologians of the nineteenth century.

The watchword of the Reformation, *Sola Scriptura*—Scripture alone— was accompanied by a conviction that Scripture, to quote Martin Luther,

---

20 See especially Rogers and McKim, *The Authority and Interpretation of the Bible: An Historical Approach* (Harper and Row, San Francisco 1979). They distinguished between the function of the Scriptures, to present the true gospel, and the form in which the message is carried. This is a false dichotomy that has more recently been used by John H Walton in his *The Lost World* trilogy (IVP Academic 2010) to re-interpret the text of Genesis 1–3.

'never erred'. This was written in contrast to the church Fathers who, 'as everyone knows' could make mistakes.[21]

Unfortunately, Luther sat loosely to this at times, as is evident in his commentary on Zechariah in 1528, when he raised the question why Matthew should attribute Zechariah 11:13 to Jeremiah (see Matthew 27:9) and concluded with the possibility that Matthew 'is not quite correct about the name.' Elsewhere, however, he maintains, 'It is impossible that Scripture should contradict itself; it only appears so to senseless and obstinate hypocrites.' Luther also claimed that 'One letter, even a single title of Scripture, means more to us than heaven and earth. Therefore, we cannot permit even the most minute change.'

Slackness in Luther's occasional comment was due, not to a low view of scriptural accuracy, but to carelessness at a time when hardly anyone was taking issue with a Bible free from error. In his debate with the Dutch theologian and ardent Roman Catholic, Desiderius Erasmus, the issue was not the inerrancy of the Bible, but its clarity. The reliability of the Bible was in fact the one thing that both Luther and his Catholic opponents, Desiderius Erasmus and John Eck, had in common. Famously, at his defence before Charles V at Worms in 1521, Luther declared that his conscience was held captive to the Word of God, the Scriptures.

The sixteenth century French Reformer, John Calvin, was clear in his claim that the Bible is the 'pure word of God' and 'the infallible rule of his holy truth.'[22] Edward Dowey, an opponent of inerrancy, admits, 'To Calvin the theologian, an error in Scripture is unthinkable.'[23] Calvin would insist on the discipline of harmonizing apparently contradictory passages, and even allow for the occasional 'copyist error', but none of this challenged his firm belief in the absolute trustworthiness of all Scripture statements. Even the Matthew 27:9 passage, that Luther dismissed as 'not

---

21 Luther's Works ed.Pelikan and Lehmann. (Fortress Press, Philadelphia 1966), Vol. 32, p. 11.
22 For an examination and defence of Calvin's position, see John D Woodbridge in *Biblical Authority*, noted above, pp. 56–63.
23 Edward Downey, *The Knowledge of God in Calvin's Theology* (Columbia University Press 1952), pp. 104–105.

quite correct', Calvin resolves by assuming the name of Jeremiah 'crept in' through a copyist's error.

In his detailed summary of Christian theology, Calvin affirmed, 'Nor is it sufficient to believe that God is true, and cannot lie or deceive, unless you feel firmly persuaded that every word which proceeds from him is sacred, inviolable truth.'[24] Elsewhere he insisted that everything written by the prophets was fulfilled in Christ and that they would not be able to write like this unless 'the Spirit of Christ went before, and in a manner dictated words to them.'[25] In his commentary on the pastoral letters of Paul, Calvin asserted, 'the Law and the Prophets are not a doctrine delivered according to the will and pleasure of men, but dictated by the Holy Spirit.'[26] Calvin is not here promoting the 'dictation' theory that we described earlier. In the short preface to his *Harmony of the Gospels*, Calvin is clear that Mark, for example, 'committed nothing to writing, but as the Holy Spirit directed him and guided his pen.'

Later Reformers and Puritans followed the same line but with one noticeable difference. Until the end of the seventeenth century there was little dispute among either Catholics or Protestants regarding biblical infallibility. The eloquent John Eck advised his friend: 'Listen, dear Erasmus, do you suppose any Christian will patiently endure to be told that the evangelists in their Gospels made mistakes?'[27] and Archbishop James Ussher calculated the year of creation as 4004 BC on the basis of the absolute reliability of biblical dates. However, with the Age of Enlightenment, free-thinking led to scepticism, and the Protestants began to tighten their terms of reference. They insisted that the infallibility of the Scriptures related to the original autographs and not to any particular translation.

William Whitaker, a Cambridge scholar, published his *A Disputation on Holy Scripture* in 1588. He believed unquestionably in biblical inerrancy

---

24 John Calvin, *Institutes of the Christian Religion*. Trans. Henry Beveridge. (James Clark & Co London 1962), 3.2.6.

25 As above, 4.8.8.

26 John Calvin, *Commentary on the Epistles to Timothy, Titus, and Philemon* trans. William Pringle. (Calvin Translation Society, Edinburgh 1856), p. 219.

27 Johann Maier Von Eck 2 February 1518, *The Correspondence of Erasmus* (University of Toronto Press 1979), Letter 769.

and he demonstrated that this was the view of the Church Fathers in the early centuries. Whitaker claimed, 'We must maintain intact the authority of Scripture in such a sense as not to allow that anything is therein delivered otherwise than the most perfect truth required.' Whitaker was a typical Puritan and believed that this infallibility related, not to any translation (he had in mind the Latin *Vulgate* of Jerome), but to the original documents written by the biblical writers. He was followed in this by William Ames in *Marrow of Sacred Divinity* in 1624.

The Protestant declarations of faith laid special emphasis on the wholly reliable Scriptures. The *Westminster Confession of Faith*, drawn up in 1643, expressed the position on this subject of all the Reformers and Puritans, of whatever churchmanship. The Old Testament in Hebrew and the New Testament in Greek: 'being immediately inspired by God, and by his singular care and providence kept pure in all ages, are therefore authentical.'[28]

The Baptist Confession of Faith (1689) claimed the Old and New Testaments 'were immediately inspired by God and were kept pure through subsequent ages by his singular care and providence.' Consequently, we have 'full persuasion and assurance of the infallible truth of Scripture and its divine authority'.[29]

Thomas Watson, in his *A Body of Divinity* published in the latter years of the seventeenth century, could have been writing for all the Puritans: 'The letter of Scripture has been preserved, without any corruption, in the original tongue. The Scriptures were not corrupted before Christ's time, for then Christ would not have sent the Jews to them. He said "Search the Scriptures." He knew these sacred springs were not muddied with human fancies.'[30]

By the eighteenth century, evangelicals were in no doubt. John Wesley, the Methodist preacher and evangelist, wrote in his diary for August 24, 1776: 'Nay, if there be any mistakes in the Bible, there may as well be a thousand. If there be one falsehood in that book, it did not come from the

---

28 The *Westminster Confession of Faith* 1:8.
29 The Baptist Confession of Faith (1689) on The Holy Scriptures 5 and 8.
30 Thomas Watson, *A Body of Divinity: of the Scriptures*, II.2.

God of truth.' He spoke for all the evangelical preachers during the Great Awakening of that century.

A century later the lines were being tightened as pseudo-scientific theories of origins undermined a trust in the Bible and liberal criticism challenged its authority. Dean Burgon delivered the Bampton lectures at Oxford in 1860–61 and lamented that it was necessary to 'defend the very inspiration of God's Word.' He declared, 'I believe that God's Word must be absolutely infallible' and he even used the phrase that it 'cannot err'.[31]

Although divided on this issue, the Church of Rome has accepted inerrancy since the Council of Trent from 1545. In 1965 Pope Paul VI confirmed, 'Since everything asserted by the inspired authors or sacred writers must be held to be asserted by the Holy Spirit, it follows that the books of Scripture must be acknowledged as teaching solidly, faithfully and without error that truth which God wanted put into sacred writings for the sake of salvation.'[32] Liberals within the church fastened onto that last phrase to suggest Scripture is not necessarily reliable on matters not relating to salvation.

A A Hodge and B B Warfield, the Princeton theologians of the late nineteenth and early twentieth century, were no inventors of new things when they spelt out the detail of biblical inerrancy and offered clear scriptural reasons for the doctrine; they were simply following a long history of mainstream Christianity. Warfield was correct in declaring that biblical inerrancy was 'The settled faith of the universal church of God ... The assured persuasion of the people of God from the first planting of the church until today.'[33]

Before his death in 1946, Professor Kirsopp Lake of Harvard University was totally opposed to the evangelical view of inerrancy—he referred to it as 'Fundamentalist'. He can be permitted the final word on this

---

31 J W Burgon, *Inspiration and Interpretation: Seven Sermons Before the University of Oxford in 1860–61, Being an answer to a volume entitled* 'Essays and Reviews'. (Oxford 1861), pp.123 and 43. The 'Essays and Reviews' were a liberal attack on the reliability of the Bible by seven clergymen.

32 *Dogmatic Constitution on Divine Revelation, Dei Verbum.* Solemnly promulgated by his Holiness Pope Paul VI on November 18, 1965. Chapter III.11.

33 Warfield, *The Inspiration and Authority of the Bible*, p.106.

question of whether the evangelical doctrine of inspiration is a recent invention: 'It is we [the liberals] who have departed from the tradition… The Bible and the whole *corpus theologicum* [body of theology] of the church is on the Fundamentalist side.'[34]

---

34 Kirsopp Lake, *The Religion of Yesterday and Tomorrow* (Boston 1926), pp. 61–62.

3. Jesus and his Bible— learning from the Master

How Jesus used the Old Testament and what this teaches us about his view of its authority.

The Bible for Jesus and the Jews was the Hebrew Scriptures (our Old Testament). See Book 3 chapter 2 in this series for the Jews and their Bible. Whatever doubts some may have concerning the value and trustworthiness of the Old Testament, those doubts were not shared by Jesus. A young man asked how he could obtain eternal life, and he was directed to the Old Testament (Matthew 19:16–22). A lawyer questioned Jesus about the law, and in reply he quoted directly from the Old Testament (Matthew 22:34–40). The Pharisees tried to trap him with hard moral questions about divorce, and they also were directed to the Old Testament (Matthew 19:3–6). Jesus used it to introduce himself (Luke 4:16–21), to fight Satan (Luke 4:1–12), to silence his enemies (Matthew 15:1–9), to instruct his hearers (John 6:25–34), to warn his disciples (Matthew 26:31) and to teach salvation (John 3:14). He used the Old Testament on the cross (Matthew 27:46) and after his resurrection (Luke 24:27). Jesus constantly quoted it and without question accepted its accuracy and authority.

Echoes of the Old Testament in the teaching of Jesus

The Gospels record direct quotations by Jesus from at least thirty-six different passages taken from thirteen Old Testament books. In addition, there are many more occasions when he referred to the Old Testament but did not quote the actual words. These indirect references or allusions are like the colourful threads in a piece of cloth. They are woven into his teaching so regularly that they help to make it the strong and attractive material that it is. Without such an accurate knowledge of the Old

Testament as Jesus and his hearers possessed, we can often miss these threads. For example: 'As soon as the grain is ripe, he puts the sickle to it, because the harvest has come' (Mark 4:29) reflects Joel 3:13 which reads: 'Swing the sickle, for the harvest is ripe.' Similarly, the phrases 'The meek ... will inherit the earth' in Matthew 5:5, and 'the pure in heart' in verse 8, are clearly reflections of Psalm 37:11 and Psalm 73:1. The parable in Matthew 21:33–41 is his application of Isaiah 5, and the terrible warning of Luke 19:44 echoes Psalm 137. In a single verse in Matthew 24:31, there are allusions to Exodus 19:16; Zechariah 2:6; 9:14; Daniel 7:2 and Deuteronomy 4:32.

No one who has any knowledge of the Old Testament can doubt that the thinking of Jesus was full of its words and phrases. He used them indirectly or directly, and never did he give his approval to anything other than the words of the Old Testament. Most of the direct quotations were introduced by a special phrase that underlined the authority of what he was about to say. In particular, he used the phrase 'It is written' on eighteen different occasions. When Jesus employed this phrase, or other phrases such as 'the Scriptures', 'the Law', 'the Prophets' and 'the Law and the Prophets', he was always introducing the Old Testament. He never used these phrases except to refer to the Old Testament.

In contrast to the relative simplicity of the Old Testament law, the Jewish rabbis, the religious teachers of Jesus' day, had added six hundred and thirteen laws of their own to God's law. Two hundred and forty-eight of these were positive and three hundred and sixty-five were negative. Many of them were petty in the extreme.

The Jewish *Talmud* is a collection of writings and discussions over the centuries by the rabbis; it was finally compiled sometime before AD 800. In the time of Jesus they were known as the *Traditions of the Elders*. They have been described as combining law reports (a Rabbinical 'Hansard'), notes of a theological debating club, anecdotes and quaint sayings and legends.[35] For a modern reader they are dull and finicky, and on the subject

---

35 Alfred Edersheim, *The Life and Times of Jesus the Messiah* (Pickering and Inglis, London 1959), Vol. 1, pp. 98–108.

of the Sabbath, pages of detail lay down what can and cannot be done, worn, carried and eaten on the seventh day. One rabbi is alleged to have spent two and a half years studying one chapter alone.

In trying to decide what 'burden' a man could or could not carry on the Sabbath, the rabbis concluded that a forbidden burden would be equal to the weight of one dried fig; but two halves of a dried fig could be carried in two journeys. A woman must not wear a band in her hair on the Sabbath because she may be tempted to remove it to show her friends 'thereby becoming guilty of carrying moveable property.' Similarly, a 'Sabbath day's journey' was two thousand cubits (just under one mile) from a man's 'dwelling place', but if the day before the Sabbath he placed two meals at the end of the two thousand cubits then he could proceed for another two thousand, for those meals were considered a 'dwelling place'. If a man wished to move a sheaf on his field, which was clearly labour, he had only to place a common utensil like a spoon on top and, to move the spoon, he would have to move the sheaf also.[36] The crowning folly was the serious instruction that if a man kept a hen for the benefit of her eggs and she foolishly laid one on the Sabbath, he could not eat it because the hen was working since laying eggs was her occupation; however, if he was fattening her for the table and she laid an egg on the Sabbath, he could eat it because that was not her chief occupation!

Jesus gave no authority to such nonsense as this, and never at any time did he discuss or quote approvingly the teaching of the rabbis. On a more serious note, he refused to accept the way the Pharisees misinterpreted and abused the Hebrew Scriptures. Jesus never introduced Jewish laws or traditions with those special phrases he reserved for Scripture alone.

In Matthew 4:4 Jesus reminded Satan of the value of the whole of Scripture: 'Man does not live on bread alone, but on every word that comes from the mouth of God.' In fact, he was quoting from Deuteronomy 8:3, but it is particularly important to notice what this verse actually says. In the first place, God used the singular 'word', not 'words', and then added 'every' to reinforce his point. Jesus was prepared to accept the authority

---

36 Edersheim, Vol. 2, pp. 56–59 for some interesting examples of this.

of every single word that God had given. In the second place, these words are described as coming 'from the mouth of God'. It is this that gave the words of Scripture their special authority. We could hardly have expected a clearer statement of inspiration than this, for the phrase 'comes from the mouth of God' is only another way of explaining the word *theopneustos*, 'God-breathed', found in 2 Timothy 3:16 and which we discussed in the previous chapter. In this verse, Jesus accepted without question that every word of Scripture had come from God. This is a belief in verbal inspiration

Although there is some debate today over the continuing relevance, or otherwise, of the Old Testament Law for the Christian, it is clear that for Jesus it stood for all time; we may debate what this means, but it cannot be denied that in Matthew 5:17–19 he emphasized the eternal and binding authority of Scripture:

'Do not think that I have come to abolish the Law or the Prophets; I have not come to abolish them but to fulfil them. I tell you the truth, until heaven and earth disappear, not the smallest letter, not the least stroke of a pen, will by any means disappear from the Law until everything is accomplished. Anyone who breaks one of the least of these commandments and teaches others to do the same will be called least in the kingdom of heaven, but whoever practises and teaches these commands will be called great in the kingdom of heaven.'

Here, Jesus warned against 'abolishing' or cancelling the law. The word refers to loosening the force of a law and making it not binding. Whether by the word 'fulfil', Jesus meant that he would carry it out to the letter or complete its requirements, is not our concern here, the fact is that for him, in some sense the law was unbreakable and binding.

The way Jesus used the Old Testament

In 1934 Rudolf Bultmann wrote in his book *Jesus and the Word*: 'Jesus agreed always with the scribes of his time in accepting without question the authority of the [Old Testament] Law... Jesus did not attack the Law but assumed its authority and interpreted it.'[37] Bultmann was a New

---

37 Rudolf Bultmann, *Jesus and the Word*, p. 61.

Testament scholar who denied the miracles recorded in the Bible, and most of its history—the crucifixion was history but the resurrection was a myth. Yet he was compelled to admit that, although he personally did not accept the inerrancy of Scripture, it is plain that Jesus did. Here are some examples of the way Jesus emphasized the authority of the Old Testament:

- 'God said, "Honour your father and mother…"' (Matthew 15:4). In quoting from Exodus Jesus did not say, 'Moses said', but 'God said'.

- In Matthew 19:4–5 he introduced the words of Genesis 2:24 and included the phrase: 'The Creator…said'. However, in Genesis the words are not specifically given as the words of the Creator. Bultmann would conclude they are merely the words of the human author, but Jesus claimed that they are the words of God.

- Quoting from Psalm 110:1, Jesus commented, 'David himself, speaking by the Holy Spirit declared…' (Mark 12:36).

- When he claimed, 'The Scripture cannot be broken' (John 10:34–35), Jesus used the same word that is found in Matthew 5:19, 'Anyone who breaks one of the least of these commandments.' In John 10:34 the quotation from Psalm 82:6 is introduced by the phrase: 'Is it not written in your Law…?' Similarly, in John 15:25 a quotation from Psalm 35:19 is referred to as written in the Law. The Psalms were therefore given the same authority as the Law that came through Moses.

- Three times Jesus countered Satan's temptations in Matthew 4:1–10 with the response: 'It is written.' He then quoted from Psalm 91 and Deuteronomy 6. For Jesus, when Scripture speaks there is nothing more to be said.

- However, the stress that he was prepared to lay upon a word, or even the use of a particular tense, in the Old Testament is significant evidence of his commitment to the verbal authority of the Old Testament. In Matthew 22:32, when challenged by the Sadducees on the question of the resurrection, Jesus did not hesitate to quote from Exodus 3:6 where the tense 'I am' was crucial to the conclusion that God is the God not of the dead but of the living. See the previous chapter for more on these examples of 'verbal' inspiration.

- A more elaborate illustration of this is found in John 10:34–36: 'Jesus answered them, "Is it not written in your Law, 'I have said you are gods'? If he called them 'gods', to whom the word of God came—and the Scripture cannot be broken—what about the one whom the Father set apart as his very own and sent into the world? Why then do you accuse me of blasphemy because I said, 'I am God's Son'?' Here Jesus reminded his hearers that the word 'god' was sometimes given to those who represented God—see for example Exodus 4:16 and 7:1 where God told Moses: 'I have made you as if you were God' to Pharaoh. The whole argument of Christ in this passage depended upon the trustworthiness of the Hebrew Scriptures even to the detail of the chosen word *elohim* (God).

Did Jesus ever contradict the Old Testament?

Six times in Matthew 5:21–43 Jesus made reference to the teaching of the Pharisees that, whilst borrowing from the Old Testament, they either misquoted or misapplied the text. His introductory phrases: 'You have heard that it was said' and 'It has been said', clearly indicate that it is not the Scriptures that are in his focus, but the Pharisaic abuse of them. In these instances, it may appear that Jesus was contradicting the Old Testament statements. However, he had already underlined the eternal value of the law (vs 17–19) and he is not so foolish as to contradict himself in the next breath.

Jesus was saying: 'You have so abused the Scriptures out of context that you have turned God's law into your own traditions; you have used God's words but have completely missed what God was saying. I will not therefore say of your laws, "It is written" but, "You have said".'

In the same way, the reader could take six words from the first paragraph of this section and claim that the author has stated, 'Jesus was contradicting the Old Testament.' Those are, in fact, my words, but on their own that is certainly not my meaning. No one can claim the authority of God when they take his words and wrest them out of context, forcing them to say something that God never intended and then adding their own words to it. That is what the Pharisees were doing; whilst the Scriptures certainly encourage 'Love your neighbour' (Leviticus 19:18), they do not add 'and hate your enemy'.

The way Jesus used the history of the Old Testament

Some may agree with all that has been said so far in this chapter, but then point out that we can accept our Lord's view of the authority of Scripture without admitting the accuracy of every historical detail. The argument is that the moral teaching and doctrine are infallible, but the history is open to error. It is that false distinction between *function* (what truth is being presented) and *form* (how the truth is presented). The word 'myth' is often used in this context. Theologians often use the word 'myth' to refer to a story that is invented to illustrate a theological or religious truth. Many insist that although much of the Bible 'history' is mythical (not historical) they are nevertheless true. By this they mean that the stories may be loosely based upon historical facts, or even invented, but their message and purpose is to tell us important truths about God.

However, our concern here is not what liberal theologians think about the stories of the Old Testament, but what Jesus thought of them. Was he teaching deep spiritual truths in stories that have little or no fact in history? It is true that in Christ's day the Jews were fond of making up stories, but nowhere do we find him using those stories. The Old Testament is written as plain history and that is exactly how Jesus used it. Not once did he cast the smallest doubt upon the historical facts of the accounts to which he referred. In every Old Testament story used by Christ two things should be noticed:

JESUS NEVER DOUBTED THE HISTORICAL ACCURACY OF THE ACCOUNT

Those who deny that Jesus was God will maintain that, as a man, he was as ignorant of the true facts as were the Jews themselves. This attack is directed towards the character of Jesus himself. If he was who he claimed to be, he could not be in error, and his endorsement of the Old Testament records is highly significant. On the other hand, if he was not God then it follows that nothing he said can be fully trusted, because his central claim to be God would be the claim of a fool or a deceiver (whether knowingly or not). He was either deceived or deceiving—a fool or a rogue; either way we could not wholly trust anything he said.

On the other hand, even if he was truly God, Jesus took upon himself certain limitations when he came to earth. For example, he could only be in one place at a time, and he required food and sleep and could feel pain. More important still, on his own admission, he consulted with his heavenly Father before he spoke: 'These words you hear are not my own; they belong to the Father who sent me' (John 14:24 see also John 8:26,40). Similarly, he limited his knowledge on earth to that which he needed to know and admitted that he did not know the time of the end of the age: 'No one knows about that day or hour, not even the angels in heaven, nor the Son, but only the Father' (Matthew 24:36). Is it not therefore reasonable to conclude that Christ did not know the truth about the Old Testament history either?

The answer to this is that the only limitation of knowledge that our Lord ever admitted during his earthly ministry, was the time of the end of the world. But this did not involve him in any falsehood either intentionally or unintentionally, knowingly or ignorantly. To suggest that Christ was ignorant of the historical facts behind Old Testament stories, and therefore continued to relate legend as if it was history, makes him party to untruths, whether intentionally or not. It attacks the character of the Messiah and his teaching to suggest that he ignorantly taught untruth while he was claiming to be 'the way and the truth and the life' (John 14:6). Besides, he claimed to be 'a man who has told you the truth that I heard from God' (John 8:40), and to question the accuracy of his words therefore challenges the reliability of both the Father and the Son.

It is sometimes argued that Jesus merely accommodated himself to the ideas of the Jews around him. He knew the Old Testament was largely myth, and that the recorded history was inaccurate; however, it suited his purpose not to attack the Jewish view of the Old Testament but simply to base his teaching upon it. His teaching is therefore truth even if the history he quoted is wrong. This is the least defensible position of all, for it makes Christ intentionally party to a lie. We can hardly be expected to trust his words if he gave the clear impression that he believed something to be true which he knew perfectly well to be wrong. We are left wondering where else he has misled us in areas where even modern scholars have not yet found him out?

JESUS ALWAYS USED THE OLD TESTAMENT TO TEACH IMPORTANT TRUTHS

In every instance of his use of Old Testament history, Jesus was not merely retelling stories to amuse his hearers, he was seeking to prove important Christian truths. In most cases, the Old Testament account was not simply used as an illustration, but as the authority for the point he wished to make. If the stories were false, how can we trust the teaching? You cannot prove a truth through the medium of a lie.

In responding to a question by the Pharisees on divorce, Jesus pointed them back to the creation account to stress that marriage is between one woman and one man and is intended for life (Matthew 19:4–5 compare Genesis 1:27; 2:24.) The thrust of his claim is entirely lost if that account in Genesis is no more than a 'myth'.

To show that his resurrection would be the greatest sign of his authority, Christ compared it with Jonah's submarine experience: 'For as Jonah was three days and three nights in the belly of a huge fish, so the Son of Man will be three days and three nights in the heart of the earth.' (Matthew 12:40). For Jesus, this story is not merely an illustration of the resurrection, it is a type of the resurrection. He is claiming from the account of Jonah, which none of his hearers would have doubted, that as the prophet came back from three days in the fish, so the Son of Man would certainly come back from the dead. If the story of Jonah and the fish is not historically true, then the resurrection may not be true either.

Similarly, in Matthew 12:41 Jesus used Jonah's preaching to Nineveh, and the repentance of that city, to warn his hearers that one day those very people in Nineveh would stand in judgement upon all who reject the gospel of Christ. One thing is certain: however Jonah arrived at Nineveh,

Jesus must have believed that a real prophet called Jonah preached to the Assyrian king Ashur-dan III and his people in Nineveh, and they must have repented. Otherwise, Jesus' serious warning about judgement was based upon a prophet who never lived, and a people who never heard the preaching he therefore did not give and who therefore did not respond to the warning they never received! This has as much value as a prosecution lawyer, in order to secure the conviction of an innocent man, inventing a story of a crime that was never committed.

To illustrate Christ's constant use of Old Testament history, here is a list. Notice that in each instance he is not simply telling a story, but illustrating or proving a significant issue.

Reference	History	Old Testament reference	Teaching
Matthew 19:4–5	Adam and Eve	Genesis 1:27; 2:24	Marriage
Luke 11:51	Cain and Abel	Genesis 4:8	Judgement
Luke 17:26–27	Noah and the flood	Genesis 6–8	Second coming of Christ
John 8:56–58	Abraham	Genesis 15–25	Deity and eternity of Christ
Luke 17:28–32; 10:12	Sodom, Gomorrah and Lot's wife	Genesis. 19	Second coming of Christ
Matthew 8:11	Isaac and Jacob	Genesis 25	Heaven and hell
Mark 7:9–10	Moses and the Ten Commandments	Exodus 20:12 Leviticus 20:9	Family duty
John 6: 31–51	The manna in the wilderness	Exodus 16	Eternal life
John 3:14	The serpent of brass	Numbers 21	Salvation
Mark 2:25–26	David and the consecrated bread	1 Samuel 21	Sabbath

Matt. 12:42	Solomon and the Queen of Sheba	1 Kings 10	Judgement
Luke 4:25–26	Elijah and the widow of Zarephath	1 Kings 17	Miracles
Luke 4:27	Elisha and Naaman	2 Kings 5	Miracles
Luke 11:51	The murder of Zechariah	2 Chronicles 24	Judgement
Matthew 12:39–41	Jonah and the fish	Jonah	Resurrection and judgement

The way Jesus applied the Old Testament to himself

At the beginning of his ministry, Jesus sat in the synagogue at Nazareth, quoted two verses from Isaiah 61 and declared, 'Today this Scripture is fulfilled in your hearing' (Luke 4:16–21). Later, whilst he was teaching in the temple courts, he quoted the first verse of Psalm 110 and challenged his listeners to explain who it was that David was writing about. He himself spelt out David's clear implication: if David called the Messiah 'my Lord' then the Christ (Messiah) must be much more than simply a descendant of the great Israelite king himself.

At the end of his earthly ministry, Jesus walked beside two unhappy disciples on the road to Emmaus. They had heard of the crucifixion but could hardly believe in the resurrection. All their hopes were gone. The stranger began by rebuking their unbelief. He told them that they should have known that the Old Testament prophets spoke of the Messiah and that therefore it was inevitable that the Christ would suffer as he had. Then he opened the Scriptures: 'And beginning with Moses and all the Prophets, he explained to them what was said in all the Scriptures concerning himself' (Luke 24:25–27). He might have said only, 'Here I am, alive!', and shown them his hands and side, but he chose rather to persuade them with the authority of Scripture.

A short while later, he did the same with the rest of the disciples: 'This is what I told you while I was still with you: Everything must be fulfilled that is written about me in the Law of Moses, the Prophets and the Psalms... He told them, "This is what is written..."' (Luke 24:44–47).

Repeatedly, Jesus asserted that the Old Testament Scriptures foretold the details of his life and death—for example, Mark 14:27,49 and John 13:18; 17:12. His chief use of the Old Testament was set before the Jews in two simple phrases: 'These are the Scriptures that testify about me... Moses wrote about me' (John 5:39, 46). Jesus based the authority of his life and ministry upon the authority and inerrancy of the Old Testament Scriptures. It is no wonder, therefore, that Jesus Christ claimed that ignorance of Scripture was the chief cause for ignorance about himself (Matthew 22:29). Once again, the choice was clear: either Jesus was correct in asserting that the Old Testament was a preparation for his own entrance into the world, or he was deliberately deceiving his hearers, or else he was himself grossly deceived.

It is the deliberate fulfilment by Jesus of Old Testament Scriptures like this that compel every reader to decide whether Jesus was really who he claimed to be or whether he was a blasphemous con man. As C S Lewis once commented, 'Either this man was, and is, the Son of God, or else a madman or something worse. You can shut him up for a fool, you can spit at him and kill him as a demon or you can fall at his feet and call him Lord and God, but let us not come with any patronizing nonsense about his being a great human teacher. He has not left that open to us. He did not intend to.'[38]

---

38 C S Lewis in *Mere Christianity*.

4. The apostles and their Bible—what Scriptures did the apostles use?

How the apostles used the Old Testament and what they believed about its authority?

Writing in *Revelation and the Bible*, Roger Nicole counted in the New Testament 224 direct quotations from the Old Testament introduced by such definite phrases as 'Scripture says,' or 'It is written'. In addition he finds seven occasions when a second quotation follows on from the first, nineteen occasions when a summary or paraphrase is used rather than a direct quotation, and forty-five when no claim to be quoting from the Old Testament is made but where a passage is clearly in mind. Nicole maintains that, if anything, this underestimates the number.[39] However, it gives us 295 references to the Old Testament contained in 352 verses of the New Testament. That is nearly four and a half per cent of the total number of verses in the New Testament, or one verse in every twenty-two and a half! Only nine books of the Old Testament are not quoted in the New Testament: Ruth, Judges, Song of Solomon, Ecclesiastes, Esther, Ezra, Nehemiah and 1 and 2 Chronicles.

In the light of these frequent references to the Hebrew Scriptures, it is particularly interesting that in the New Testament there is not one quotation from a book of the *Apocrypha*. The *Apocrypha* is a group of Jewish religious books that were written after the close of the Old Testament and before the start of the New Testament. Historically,

---

39 Roger Nicole, 'New Testament use of the Old Testament'. Carl F H Henry ed, *Revelation and the Bible* (Tyndale Press, London 1959), pp.137–138.

therefore, it is placed between Malachi and Matthew. In Book 3 chapter 2 of this series the *Apocrypha* is discussed in more detail.

This constant use of the Old Testament is very impressive and we must ask the question: How did the apostles use the Old Testament? In the previous chapter we saw Jesus' use of it, but what did the Master's men think of it when they wrote their letters to the young churches?

God is considered the author of the Old Testament

On fifty-six occasions, the New Testament refers to God as the author of the Old Testament, and even where the human writer is known, divine authorship is occasionally stated instead. Two significant examples come from the letter to the Hebrews:

- In Hebrews 1:5–13 quotations are taken from 2 Samuel 7:14 and Psalms 2:7; 104:4; 45:6–7; 102:25–27; 110:1. The human writers are ignored entirely and five times the apostle introduces a quotation with the phrase: 'He [or God] says'.

- The same writer quoted from Jeremiah 31 with the simple introduction: 'The Holy Spirit also testifies to us about this...' (Hebrews 10:15).

Similarly, on the day of Pentecost, Peter quoted from Joel 2:28 and claimed '"In the last days", God says, "I will pour out my Spirit on all people..."' (Acts 2:17).

Divine authorship is added to the human writer

The human writers are not always ignored. The apostles were aware of the men who wrote the Old Testament, and yet when they referred to them they often felt the need to emphasize the divine authorship as well. Here are four examples:

- In Acts 1:16 Peter quoted from Psalm 41:9 and he introduced the verse in this way: 'Brothers, the Scripture had to be fulfilled, which the Holy Spirit spoke long ago through the mouth of David...'

- Similarly, in Acts 4:25 the apostles prayed, 'You spoke by the Holy Spirit through the mouth of your servant, our father David...'

- In Acts 28:25 Paul introduced Isaiah 6:9–10 to his Jewish hearers with the words: 'The Holy Spirit spoke the truth to your forefathers when he said through Isaiah the prophet ...'

- In Romans 9:25 Paul began a quotation from Hosea 2:23 with: 'As he [God] says in Hosea...'

There can therefore be no doubt that these apostles understood the words of the Old Testament writers to be those of God the Holy Spirit speaking through men. Peter's reference to the Spirit speaking through the mouth of David reveals their acceptance of 'inspiration' in the way we have earlier defined it (2 Peter 1:20–21), and the reason why Paul could write of the Scriptures as 'God-breathed' (*theopneustos* in 2 Timothy 3:16).

Scripture is identified with God

The phrases 'Scripture says' or 'the Law says' are often used when, in the Old Testament passage, we are told that God is speaking. The implication is that whenever Scripture speaks, it is God speaking; these expressions are therefore the same as, 'God says'.

- In Romans 7:7 Paul wrote, 'The Law ... said, "Do not covet",' and he then quoted from Exodus 20:17. However, Exodus 20:1 distinctly records, 'God spoke all these words.'

- Paul introduced the words of God to Pharaoh found in Exodus 9:16 with the phrase: 'The Scripture says to Pharaoh...' (Romans 9:17).

- He similarly claimed, 'The Scripture ... announced the gospel in advance to Abraham' (Galatians 3:8) and then continued by quoting Genesis 12:3 where we are told in verse 1: 'The Lord said to Abram...'

These are only three of many examples and the conclusion must be that 'Scripture says', 'the Law says', and 'God says' are all the same in the apostle's mind.[40]

The term 'law' is used for the whole of the Old Testament

Although the phrase 'the Law says' is the same as 'God says' in the minds of the apostles, the term 'Law' does not cover merely the Ten Commandments. Everything in the Old Testament has the force of law in the sense of its authoritative claim upon the Israelites. Although the Jews generally divided their Scriptures (our Old Testament) into three parts—the Law, the Writings and the Prophets—they frequently referred to the whole of the Old Testament as 'the Law'. Therefore, when Jesus was speaking to the Jews and quoting from Psalm 82, which was part of the Writings, he could say, 'Is it not written in your Law?' (John 10:34). This was the view of the apostles also; every part of the Old Testament carried the authority of God's law.

- In Romans 3:19 Paul placed a number of Scriptures under the general heading of 'Law', but he had just quoted from five Psalms and the prophet Isaiah.

- Similarly, in 1 Corinthians 14:21 the apostle claimed, 'In the Law it is written...' and then continued with a quotation from Isaiah 28:11–12.

The Old Testament Scriptures are the 'words' of God

On two occasions the Greek word *logion* (word) is used with reference to the Old Testament. This word *logion* is similar to, though not identical with, the more commonly used word *logos*, but it has a very special meaning. Outside the Bible pagan writers often used it to refer to an utterance from the gods. Some of our English versions translate it by the word 'oracle'. In Acts 7:38 Stephen claimed that the Ten Commandments came by Moses, who 'received living *words* to pass on to us', and in

---

40 A detailed discussion of this will be found in Benjamin B Warfield, *The Inspiration and Authority of the Bible* (Presbyterian and Reformed Publishing Company, Philadelphia 1948), pp. 399 on.

Romans 3:2 Paul wrote that the Jews were 'entrusted with the very *words* of God'. There are only two other uses of this word in the whole of the New Testament. In Hebrews 5:12 ('God's word') it refers to the summary of Christian doctrine and in 1 Peter 4:11 the Christian teacher is to speak 'as one speaking the very *words* of God'.

The *Septuagint* (the Greek translation of the Old Testament completed between 250 and 150 BC, and which would have been very familiar to the apostles; see Book 3 chapter 2 in this series), uses this Greek word *logion* thirty-six times to translate the Hebrew word *imrah* when it refers to the words of God. Nineteen of these are in Psalm 119, which has a direct reference to God's word in all but five of its one 176 verses. In Psalm 105:19 the *Septuagint* uses the word *logos* in the first half to refer to the words of Joseph and then *logion* in the second half (where *imrah* is in the Hebrew text) to distinguish Joseph's words from those of the LORD. Clearly the translators intended to emphasise the absolute authority of the words of the LORD. In Numbers 24:4, *logia* (translated 'words') is similarly used to translate *imrah* in order to stress the authority of the words of God. Warfield, concludes that, 'it is essentially this conception of the "unspeakable oracles of God" that is conveyed by the word in every instance of its occurrence.'[41]

Philo, the Greek-Jewish philosopher who died around AD 50, used the *Septuagint* for much of his Hebrew Scriptures study (although he was proficient in Hebrew), and he consistently used the word *logion* to refer to the sacred oracles of God which, for him, was the whole of our Old Testament.[42]

Stephen, Paul and Peter were each familiar with the *Septuagint* and the way in which *logion* was used by both sacred and pagan writers. They would therefore use the word *logion* in the same way. Many of the leaders of the church, writing shortly after the close of the New Testament, used the word *logion* in exactly this way, to refer to a sacred word from God.

---

41 See Warfield, pp. 366–371 for a full discussion on the use of *logion* in the *Septuagint* to translate *imrah*.
42 Warfield, pp. 374–375.

The Old Testament is God-given, authoritative and relevant

We should recall that from 2 Timothy 3:16 and 2 Peter 1:21 it is evident how committed the New Testament writers were to the divine authorship of the Old Testament. In addition, they were aware of the fact that everything in the Old Testament was relevant for the first century. When the New Testament used the expression 'It is written', to introduce a quotation from the Old, the writers were not merely finding a convenient way of introducing their reference; on the contrary, the phrase was significant in that it registered the fact that what follows is part of the written and unbreakable word of God. The phrase 'It is written' occurs eighty-six times in the New Testament; forty of those are in the Gospels, chiefly used by Jesus himself.

Speaking to the Jews at Pisidian Antioch, Paul quoted from Isaiah 49:6 and declared, 'This is what the Lord has commanded us' (Acts 13:47). Similarly, the writer to the Hebrews quoted Proverbs 3:11–12 and introduced it with the challenge: 'You have forgotten that word of encouragement that addresses you as sons' (Hebrews 12:5–6).

There was nothing merely historical about the Old Testament for the apostles; it was a book of authority and relevance and they placed themselves under its commands. Paul could honestly claim before the governor Felix: 'I believe everything that agrees with the Law and that is written in the Prophets...' (Acts 24:14). Similarly, he could write to the Christians at Rome: 'Everything that was written in the past was written to teach us...' (Romans 15:4).

Paul's use of the Old Testament in 1 Corinthians 15 is typical of the New Testament writers. He was concerned to demonstrate the historical fact of the physical resurrection of Christ because some in the church at Corinth had denied this. Paul had many arguments to make and many eyewitnesses to offer, but his first reason for asserting the truth of the resurrection of Christ was that it was based on the Old Testament. Christ's death and resurrection took place: 'according to the Scriptures' (vs 2–3).

How the apostles 'quoted' from the Old Testament[43]

When the New Testament writers quoted the Old Testament, they frequently used the Greek *Septuagint*. It was only natural that they should use this translation since they spoke Greek and so did all their readers. Greek was the common language of the first century Roman Empire, especially in the Middle East. In this, they had the example of their Master to follow, since Jesus also occasionally made use of the Greek translation of the Old Testament. Interestingly, in Matthew 19:5, Mark 10:8 and 1 Corinthians 6:16, both Jesus and Paul quoted from the *Septuagint* in preference to the Hebrew (Masoretic) text of Genesis 2:24 because in the phrase 'and the two will become one flesh', the words *and the two* are not found in the Hebrew, but they are in the Greek. This is a small difference, but clearly both Jesus and Paul are drawing out the true significance of the original. Occasionally one writer follows the Hebrew (Matthew 8:17 quoting from Isaiah 53:4–5) while another takes the same verse from the Greek (1 Peter 2:24).

In the light of the strong commitment that the apostles clearly had to the Old Testament Scriptures as God-given, it may seem strange that they appear often to be slack in the way they quote it. Sometimes they used the *Septuagint* in places where it was not a very precise translation of the Hebrew—and they did not bother to correct it. On other occasions, they chose to refer loosely to a passage and in so doing departed from both the Hebrew and the Greek translation. They may even have been using an alternative Greek translation.

Sometimes the New Testament writers chose the *Septuagint* because it more clearly expressed the point they wished to make. An example of this is where James' speech recorded in Acts 15:16–18 used Amos 9:11,12 from the *Septuagint*. The one difference of note is the phrase in the Hebrew text 'so that they may possess the remnant of Edom' which the Greek

---

43 On this subject of the New Testament use of Old Testament quotations see the response by Roger Nicole in *Revelation and the Bible* ed Carl F H Henry (Tyndale Press, London 1959), pp. 41–151. Also, Carson and Woodbridge editors of the symposium *Hermeneutics, Authority, and Canon* (Inter-Varsity Press, Leicester 1986), ch. 5 by Douglas Moo. And by the same editors *Scripture and Truth* (Inter-Varsity Press, 1983) by Moisés Silva, pp. 147–172.

renders 'that the remnant of men may seek the Lord'. Even though the Hebrew made the same point (ie those chosen from the Gentile nations will also come to Christ), the *Septuagint* expressed it more plainly for James' purpose.

If we accept Paul's statement in 1 Corinthians 2:13 that the apostles spoke 'in words taught by the Spirit' we shall have no difficulty in accepting the way the New Testament writers handled the Old Testament, whichever version they quoted from. The verbal inerrancy of Scripture leads us to believe that a change of words from the Hebrew to the Greek, when used by the New Testament writers, infallibly reflects the mind of God through those words. Never did the New Testament writers try to support an argument by a bad translation. Therefore, they had no need to correct the *Septuagint*, even if they had known it was not the best translation.

On the use of the *Septuagint*, see also in this series Book 4 chapter 4 'The text of the Old Testament'.

PARAPHRASING AND A FREE TRANSLATION

A preacher today will have a modern translation in front of him as he preaches. A verse he wants to refer to during his sermon may not be the best possible translation, but if it is adequate for his purpose he will not bother to correct it; to do so would divert the attention of his congregation away from his main purpose. At times a preacher may cover a whole passage of Scripture with his own free paraphrase, but this does not imply any weakness in his view of biblical inerrancy.

Romans 10:6–8 is hardly a literal quotation from Deuteronomy 30:11–14, but it is an excellent paraphrase; the apostle used that which suited his theme. Paul is only in error if it can be shown that he intended to quote exactly. In this passage, Paul quoted neither from the Hebrew nor the Greek (though he possessed both). He paraphrased loosely to draw out the meaning. Similarly, in Romans 11:8, 'God gave them a spirit of stupor', is a paraphrase of Isaiah 29:10, 'The Lord has brought over you a deep sleep.' The words that the apostles employ to give the sense of an Old Testament passage are themselves God-breathed and are therefore exactly what God intended in order to draw out an accurate meaning of the words he first gave to the Old Testament prophets.

The apostles did not assume that the *Septuagint* became an inspired translation whenever they used it; it was simply a translation, and was authoritative only in so far as it faithfully represented the original Old Testament Hebrew. Their use of it is infallible, but this does not imply infallibility in the whole or any part of the Greek translation. God can speak through a translation of his word, even though the translation may not be perfect.

In addition to this, the apostles did not have the advantages of the modern writer in the use of punctuation, quotation marks, brackets and so on; these aids did not exist in the first century. Therefore, we cannot always be sure when they stop a direct quotation and begin their own paraphrase or interpretation of an Old Testament passage. For example, Romans 3:10–12 is a free paraphrase of Psalm 14:1–3, and in the next six verses Paul sprinkles in parts of Psalm 5:9, Psalm 140:3, Psalm 10:7, Isaiah 59:7–8 and Psalm 36:1. It would be quite wrong to accuse Paul either of inaccuracies or a low view of Scripture because he chooses only to select parts of the verses.

Occasionally, the New Testament writers appear to be quoting from the Old Testament, yet part company with both the Hebrew and the Greek translation. Matthew is sometimes free in his use of the Old Testament. A comparison of Matthew 12:18–21 with Isaiah 42:1–4 illustrates this; he begins with the Hebrew, departs from both Hebrew and Greek versions in the phrase 'till he leads justice to victory' (v 20) and concludes by quoting from the Greek. Either he is quoting from an alternative Greek text or, more likely, he is part-quoting and part-paraphrasing, since he says nothing that is not in the Hebrew text.

In Ephesians 4:7–8 Paul wrote, 'But to each one of us grace has been given as Christ apportioned it. This is why it says, "When he ascended on high, he led captives in his train and gave gifts to men."' The passage Paul had in mind is Psalm 68:18 which reads: 'When you ascended on high, you led captives in your train; you received gifts from men.' Both the Hebrew and the Greek Old Testaments agree that God 'received gifts *from* men'.

Either Paul had misquoted ('and gave gifts *to* men'), which is unlikely considering his wide and deep knowledge of the Hebrew Scriptures or, as some have suggested, he is not referring to the Psalm at all—which is even less likely.

Perhaps the best explanation, suggested as long ago as 1854 by William Lee, is that Psalm 68:18 looks forward to the ascension of Christ as a result of which we bring worship (gifts) to God, and Paul emphasises that we can only do this when God gives gifts to us by his Spirit. Paul's emphasis is that as a result of the ascension of Christ each of God's people receive grace for gifts which they offer God (v 7). As Lee concludes: 'That God should *take* to himself, he must first, from the very nature of the case, *give* certain graces to man.'[44] Paul is providing a fuller sense of the Psalm by turning it to his own use.

However, what the apostles could do we must be cautious in copying. Whilst it is quite appropriate for us to paraphrase and quote loosely, providing we are accurate, it would be wholly wrong to turn a passage round, as Paul does in Ephesians 4:8, without a careful explanation of what we are doing and why. Paul himself was passing on part of the God-breathed word, and therefore his interpretation carries an authority that ours cannot.

When the apostles are apparently free in their application of an Old Testament passage, giving it a meaning that is not clearly there in the original, does this challenge the view of verbal inspiration? Even C H Dodd, who did not accept verbal inspiration, maintained that in making use of passages from the Old Testament, the apostles 'in general … remain true to the main intention of their writers'.[45] You will notice he says, 'in general'. So, what about the occasions when they are more free than we would be in the way they apply the Old Testament?

---

44 William Lee, *The Inspiration of Holy Scripture* (Hodge, Smith & Co. Dublin 3rd ed. 1864), pp. 352–354.
45 C H Dodd, *According to the Scriptures* (Nisbet, London 1952), p. 130.

A FULLER MEANING

Peter evidently set out a principle that all the New Testament writers followed, and that we should not overlook: those who wrote the Hebrew Scriptures were frequently writing more than they fully understood. They may have been writing from their own perspective and experience, but their words often had a fulfilment much wider and farther into the future than they could know. Peter expressed the principle in this way:

'Concerning this salvation, the prophets, who spoke of the grace that was to come to you, searched intently and with the greatest care, trying to find out the time and circumstances to which the Spirit of Christ in them was pointing when he predicted the sufferings of Christ and the glories that would follow. It was revealed to them that they were not serving themselves but you, when they spoke of the things that have now been told you by those who have preached the gospel to you by the Holy Spirit sent from heaven. Even angels long to look into these things' (1 Peter 1:10–12).

This must have been true of David in his detailed description of the death of the Messiah in Psalm 22, Isaiah would not necessarily have a perfect understanding of the One he was prophesying in Isaiah 53, or Joel fully appreciate his foretelling of the Holy Spirit, and Daniel would not need to understand what many of his strange visions and prophecies referred to.

If the doctrine of the Scriptures as the God-breathed word is true, then we can safely assume that where the New Testament writers understood an Old Testament passage in a less than obvious way, or applied it in a way we would hesitate to, this is because God had more light to reveal to us through the apostles. Earlier writers on this subject referred to the *sensus plenior*, which means, the 'fuller meaning' of Scripture. There is a necessary warning here to the unwary: this is not intended to give licence for foolish interpretations and applications of Scripture. Unfortunately, the Alexandrian School of interpreting Scripture, led by able men like Clement and Origen in the third century AD, often discarded the literal meaning of Scripture in favour of a highly imaginative approach. See Book 6 chapters 2 and 3 in this series on how to understand the Bible.

The apostles have provided us with an insight into a deeper or fuller meaning of the Old Testament providing new meanings for the Old.

- Even though *we* may not readily see the rock from which water came for the Jews in the wilderness as a symbol of Christ (1 Corinthians 10:1–5), clearly Paul did.

- In 1 Corinthians 15:27 the Hebrew text and the Greek translation of Psalm 8:6, both use the second person singular: '*You* put everything under his feet...', whereas Paul uses the third person 'he' (God) and 'his' (Christ). Is Paul quoting, or simply using the language of the Psalm? The answer is that in Psalm 8 we read of man in his created state before the Fall and in 1 Corinthians 15:45–47 Paul claims that Christ is the second (and last) Adam, so Psalm 8 is given a Messianic meaning by the apostle.

- Both Romans 1:17 and Galatians 3:11 quote from the Old Testament where the Hebrew text (the *Masoretic Text*) of Habakkuk 2:4 has 'The righteous will live by *his* faith', and the *Septuagint* has 'The righteous will live by *my* faith.' Paul omits both and states simply; 'The righteous will live *by faith*...' Since faith is a gift of God, he chooses to refer to it as neither belonging to God nor man. Both the Hebrew *Masoretic Text* and the Greek *Septuagint* are correct since faith, whilst a gift from God, becomes the personal expression of faith by the individual.

- In Galatians 3:16 the Hebrew and Greek word for 'seed' (as in the English also) can be either singular or plural. But Paul, by insisting upon the singular, is drawing out a deeper meaning and reading Christ as the fulfilment of God's promises through Israel (Luke 24:27).

- In 1 Timothy 5:17–18 (and 1 Corinthians 9:8–12) it is Paul's intention to encourage the churches to support financially those who lead the work. To do so he turns his readers to Deuteronomy 25:4 which forbids muzzling an ox whilst it is treading out the grain; Paul points out that this passage on the Law was not primarily about oxen, but about the support of Christian workers. That is a fuller meaning of the Scriptures.

On this basis, the apostles were correct in looking for a deeper fulfilment of many Old Testament passages than lay on the surface. C H Dodd also acknowledged that many New Testament writers took passages from the Old 'which start from their first historical intention and these lines are carried forward to fresh results'.[46] Therefore, whilst we accept the application of the New Testament writer to be under the direction of the Holy Spirit, it does not follow that this is necessarily the only application of that passage in its historical context.

It has been generally accepted, even by liberal commentators on the Bible, that however we may understand this less than precise use of the biblical text by the apostles, they all accepted without reservation that God, through the agency of the Holy Spirit, was the author of the entire Old Testament.[47]

Scriptures for every occasion

Roger Nicole summarized the apostolic use of the Old Testament: 'The New Testament writers used quotations in their sermons, in their histories, in their letters, in their prayers. They used them when addressing Jews or Gentiles, churches or individuals, friends or antagonists, new converts or seasoned Christians. They used them for argumentation, for illustration, for instruction, for documentation, for prophecy, for reproof. They used them in times of stress and in hours of mature thinking, in liberty and in prison, at home and abroad. Everywhere and always they were ready to refer to the impregnable authority of Scripture...'[48]

That is a bold assertion, but can we actually find instances to prove his claim? Here is a list of all the categories he mentions with an example in each case of how the New Testament writers made a habit of quoting the Old Testament Scriptures.

---

46 As above.
47 Roger Nicole in *Revelation and the Bible* (see above, p. 151) quotes several of these liberal commentators.
48 *Revelation and the Bible*, p. 140.

Sermons. In Peter's sermon on the Day of Pentecost, Acts 2:17–21 is a direct quotation from Joel 2:28–32. Using the same passage, Paul later applied it in a missionary context (Romans 10:13).

Histories. Stephen, immediately before his martyrdom, traced the history of Israel and he referred to Genesis, Exodus, Deuteronomy, Numbers, Isaiah, Amos and a Psalm (Acts 7).

Letters. There are quotations or allusions to the Old Testament in virtually every letter in the New Testament. As just one example, Romans 8:36 is a quotation from Psalm 44:22.

Prayers. With the arrest of Peter and John, the Christians went to prayer, and in Acts 4:24–26 they used Psalms 146:6 and 2:1.

Jews. Paul preached to the Jews at Pisidian Antioch where, according to Acts 13:33–35, 41, he referred to two Psalms, Isaiah and Habakkuk.

Gentiles. At Lystra Paul and Barnabas were mistaken for Greek gods. According to Acts 14:15, Paul enshrined Exodus 20:11 in his response.

Churches. Peter wrote to Christians scattered throughout the Roman Empire and frequently used the Old Testament to support his teaching. 1 Peter alone contains quotations from Leviticus, two Psalms, Proverbs and Isaiah.

Individuals. Paul wrote to Timothy, who was ministering at Ephesus, and in 1 Timothy 5:18 quoted from Deuteronomy 25:4.

Friends. Because of his experiences in the town, Paul must have counted the Christians at Ephesus among his closest friends. Ephesians 4:8 is a quotation from Psalm 68:18.

Antagonists. Paul faced opposition from Jewish leaders at Rome, and in Acts 28:26–27 he turned his accusers to Isaiah 6:9–10.

New converts. Galatians was probably Paul's first letter, and the young Christians were already sliding from the truth. Galatians 3 contains references to Genesis, Leviticus, Deuteronomy and Habakkuk.

Seasoned Christians. Timothy, though young, had proved himself an experienced worker. 2 Timothy 2:19 quotes from Numbers 16 and Isaiah 28.

Argumentation. The great debate at Jerusalem was settled by James, who in Acts 15:16–18 reminded the council of Amos 9.

Illustration. Paul illustrated the slavery of law and the liberty of Christ by reference to Hagar and Sarah. Galatians 4:27,30 are taken from Isaiah 54 and Genesis 21.

Instruction. Paul taught the Roman Christians about Israel and evangelism, and Romans 10 contains quotations from Leviticus, Deuteronomy, Isaiah and Joel.

Documentation. The writer to the Hebrews listed some of the great saints of the past, and his familiar eleventh chapter is packed with references to the Old Testament and contains direct quotations from Genesis 15 and 21.

Prophecy. Paul turned to the Old Testament for a prophecy of the resurrection and supported his position in 1 Corinthians 15:54–55 with quotations from Isaiah 25 and Hosea 13.

Reproof. The Hebrew Christians had forgotten the benefits of discipline, and Hebrews 12:5–6 is taken from Proverbs 3:11–12.

Stress. Peter and John were on trial before the Jewish rulers but the record of their response in Acts 4:11 is a quotation from Psalm 118.

Mature thought. Paul's letter to Rome is surely the most mature exposition of the Christian faith ever to have been written. In this letter, there are fifty-three quotations from the Old Testament, and Romans 15 alone contains quotations from three Psalms, Deuteronomy, Isaiah and 2 Samuel.

Liberty. Peter's second sermon after Pentecost was given at a time when nothing could hold the disciples back from evangelism. Acts 3:22–23 is taken from Deuteronomy 18.

Prison. John was a prisoner on the island of Patmos and his vision received there and recorded in the book of Revelation contains at least fourteen quotations and paraphrases from seven books of the Old Testament.

At home. James wrote from his home town of Jerusalem and the second chapter of his letter contains quotations from Leviticus 19; Exodus 20; Genesis 15 and Isaiah 41.

Abroad. Paul wrote 2 Corinthians from Macedonia. 2 Corinthians 6:2 is taken from Isaiah 49:8.

There can be no doubt that when Paul reminded the church at Rome: 'Everything that was written in the past was written to teach us, so that through endurance and the encouragement of the Scriptures we might have hope' (Romans 15:4), he represented the view, not only of the apostles, but of all the leaders in the first century churches. It is the Hebrew Scriptures, and those alone, that carried the full weight of divine authority, the very oracles of God.

5. Absolute authority— the prophets, Jesus and the apostles

The writers of the Old Testament, Jesus and the apostles all laid claim to the fact that they spoke with the authority of God.

In 1521, Martin Luther, stood before the Emperor Charles V, in the town of Worms in Germany. Luther was on trial for insisting upon the authority of Scripture as opposed to the traditions of men and the decrees of the popes. History records that towards the end of the debate, the German Reformer challenged his accusers: 'I am bound by the Scriptures and my conscience has been taken captive by the word of God, and I am neither able nor willing to recant, since it is neither safe nor right to act against conscience. God help me. Amen.' The trial immediately ended in confusion.

Luther was not the only one to make this stand. Even today countless millions of Christians give their liberty and lives for their confidence in this book, and gladly submit to its authority and allow it to guide them in the details of how they should live and what they should believe. But why do they do this? Those who do not believe the Bible sometimes argue that this God-given authority has been imposed upon Scripture: that is to say, the Bible never considered itself as having special and final authority, but this claim has been imposed on it as the centuries passed.

To answer this, we have seen in chapter two what the Bible teaches about its own 'inspiration' and inerrancy and how Jesus and the apostles used their Scriptures. The purpose of this chapter is to discover what the writers of the Old and New Testaments thought about their own writings. Did they believe their words carried divine authority or not? Can we justify using those two key passages in 2 Timothy 3:16 and 2 Peter 1:21 to cover the New Testament writers also?

The claim of the Old Testament

THE PROPHETS' CLAIM TO DIVINE AUTHORITY

The prophets knew themselves to be governed by the Spirit of God. Nearly four thousand times in the Old Testament—around five hundred in the first five books alone—we read such expressions as 'The LORD spoke', 'The LORD commanded' or 'The LORD said'. None of the prophets spoke on his own authority. Micah contrasted himself with the false prophets and claimed, 'But as for me, I am filled with power, with the Spirit of the Lord' (Micah 3:8). Zechariah spoke for both himself and the prophets who had come before him when he accused Israel of ignoring, 'the words that the LORD Almighty had sent by his Spirit through the earlier prophets' (Zechariah 7:12).

Even David, who was a prophet and composed many of the Old Testament psalms, declared in his dying speech: 'The Spirit of the LORD spoke through me; his word was on my tongue. The God of Israel spoke, the Rock of Israel said to me...' (2 Samuel 23:2–3).

THEIR EXPERIENCE OF RECEIVING THE MESSAGE FROM GOD

The prophets never thought of their message as originating in their own minds or with their own ideas. In fact their description of the false prophets was precisely that *they* were men who prophesied 'out of their own imagination' (Ezekiel 13:2). On the contrary, the true prophets knew that their words were given directly by God. Jeremiah described his call to the prophetic ministry in this way: 'Then the LORD reached out his hand and touched my mouth and said to me: "Now, I have put my words in your mouth..."' (Jeremiah 1:9). Isaiah recorded a similar divine preparation in Isaiah 51:16; 59:21. In the same way, God promised Moses that his successor would speak with the authority of Moses himself: 'I will raise up for them a prophet like you from among their brothers; I will put my words in his mouth, and will tell them everything I command him.'

(Deuteronomy 18:18). This verse has an ultimate fulfilment in the coming Messiah, but it also covers the immediate successors of Moses.

However we understand these claims, it is clear that the prophets were convinced that they received the words of their prophetic ministry in an unusual manner, which was completely different from the ideas that came to them in normal conversation. As a consequence, they saw themselves as God's spokesmen (Ezekiel 3:4).

Perhaps even more startling is the expression that the prophets actually *saw* their message. Whether this was a seeing with the eye or with the mind is not always clear, but what is certain is that the prophet received his message in such a vivid and convincing manner that it could be described in no other way than 'seeing'. Isaiah introduced a message with the statement: 'This is what Isaiah son of Amoz saw concerning Judah and Jerusalem' (Isaiah 2:1). Amos 1:1; Micah 1:1; Habakkuk 1:1 and Revelation 1:19 all record a similar experience.

This experience of 'seeing' his message in a vision or dream led to the prophet being called a 'seer' on at least twelve occasions in the Old Testament (see for example, 1 Samuel 9:9; Amos 7:12; and 1 Chronicles 26:28). Even in the time of Isaiah, the rebellious people were aware of the significance of this word: 'They say to the seers, "See no more visions!", and to the prophets, "Give us no more visions of what is right! Tell us pleasant things, prophesy illusions"' (Isaiah 30:10).

THEIR RESPONSIBILITY TO SPEAK ONLY THE WORDS OF GOD

Standing in this special relationship with God, the prophets could not speak beyond the words God gave them. The view of Amos was typical of all the prophets of the Lord; they knew themselves to be in an unusual relationship with God and they appreciated the solemn responsibility of this. Amos could record, 'Surely the Sovereign LORD does nothing without revealing his plan to his servants the prophets' (Amos 3:7). In consequence of this, the prophets not only had to speak the words God gave them, but were unable to say anything other than that which God commanded them. So Amos declared, 'The lion has roared—who will not fear? The Sovereign LORD has spoken—who can but prophesy?' (Amos 3:8).

Even the rebellious prophet Balaam could do no other than remind King Balak, who was trying to bribe Balaam to curse the people of Israel: 'Even if Balak gave me his palace filled with silver and gold, I could not do anything of my own accord, good or bad, to go beyond the command of the LORD—and I must say only what the LORD says' (Numbers 24:13). It is hardly surprising therefore that again and again the prophets began their message with the words 'Hear the word of the LORD' (see for example Isaiah 1:10; Jeremiah 10:1; Micah 6:1).

This clear sense of accountability to God is seen in the warnings that came through the prophets not to add to God's words. Moses passed on to the people the solemn warning from God: 'Do not add to what I command you and do not subtract from it…' (Deuteronomy 4:2). A similar warning is conveyed through Proverbs 30:6: 'Do not add to his words, or he will rebuke you and prove you a liar.'

Although there is some uncertainty about the original meaning of the Hebrew word *nabi* (prophet), it is generally agreed that it refers to a spokesman on behalf of another. David Aune, in his thorough research into the use of the idea of prophets in ancient times, concludes that across the Mediterranean world the prophet was, 'One who speaks in place of or on behalf of the god.' [49] This is illustrated in the episode recorded in Numbers 12:1–8 where Miriam and Aaron rebelled against the authority of Moses. They challenged, 'Has the LORD spoken only through Moses? Hasn't he also spoken through us?' God's reply was to remind Moses' sister and brother that he reveals himself to his prophets through visions and dreams, but that Moses stands in a special relationship with God; he was one to whom God revealed himself 'face to face'. Moses, like all the prophets, stood as a spokesman for God and should not be opposed.

This is exactly how the Jews understood the ministry of all the Old Testament writers. When Moses came down from Mount Sinai, he gathered together the elders of Israel and gave them 'all the words the LORD had commanded him to speak.' The immediate response of the

---

49 David Aune, *Prophecy in early Christianity and the Ancient Mediterranean World* (Eerdmans Publishing, Grand Rapids 1983), p. 29.

elders showed their complete trust in Moses as the voice of God: 'We will do everything the LORD has said' (Exodus 19:7–8). All through history, sincere Jews accepted this view of the Scriptures as the word of God.

THE AUTHORITY OF THE WORDS

The words of the Old Testament were all considered to have God-given authority. This thought runs throughout the Old Testament and is woven into it like the strands of a piece of cloth. Nowhere is it found more clearly than in Psalm 119, which consists of 176 verses and only five contain no direct reference to the word of God. It is not claiming too much to say that verse 160 is a summary of the Old Testament's view of itself: 'All your words are true; all your righteous laws are eternal.' As a consequence of this, there was no doubt in the minds of the Old Testament writers that every word of God was 'flawless' (Proverbs 30:5–6). The word translated 'flawless' comes from a root verb meaning 'to refine metal'. Therefore, the Greek translation uses a word meaning to burn with fire or purify. The passive use in Proverbs 30 implies that the words have been tested and proved true; because by the agency of the Holy Spirit any flaw or impurity has been taken out.

The claim of the New Testament

We examined in chapter 2 the importance of 2 Timothy 3:16 and 2 Peter 1:21; it is therefore sufficient here to remind ourselves that the first tells us *where* the Scriptures came from (from God), and the second informs us *how* they came to us (through men moved by the Holy Spirit). In their immediate context, they refer to the Old Testament because this was the Bible of the New Testament Christians. What we now need to show is that the same authority the New Testament writers saw in the Old Testament, they also claimed for themselves—and for each other.

THE CLAIMS OF THE WRITERS TO DIVINE AUTHORITY

The New Testament writers claimed to speak and write by the Holy Spirit and with the authority of God. When Paul wrote to the Corinthian Christians he found it necessary to defend his authority as an apostle against those who had refused to accept his ministry. Paul's argument was that he wrote and preached, 'not in words taught us by human wisdom, but words taught by the Spirit' (1 Corinthians 2:13). Before this is dismissed as a claim to nothing more than a wisdom a little above the average, it must not be forgotten that prior to his conversion Paul was a highly educated leader of the Jews and was immersed in the Hebrew Scriptures (Acts 22:3). He was well aware that a claim like this was almost identical to the claim of the Old Testament prophets.

In exactly the same way, Peter could encourage the young churches to: 'recall the words spoken in the past by the holy prophets and the command given by our Lord and Saviour through your apostles' (2 Peter 3:2). The translators have handled well an unusual form of Greek here; the emphasis is not that the apostles merely passed on the commands that Jesus had given during his earthly ministry, but that they now spoke with the voice of Jesus himself. A reasonable translation would be: 'the commandment of the apostles of the Lord Jesus'.

Peter not only gave equal authority to the words of the prophets and apostles, but he also declared his belief that 'our Lord and Saviour' now revealed his commands to his church through the apostles. In his first letter, Peter is even more direct. He first made the statement, familiar to many of his readers, that the Old Testament prophets spoke of the coming of Christ by the power of 'the Spirit of Christ in them'(1 Peter 1:11). Peter then turned his attention to the apostles 'who have preached the gospel to you by the Holy Spirit sent from heaven' (v 12). Clearly, then, to Peter's thinking, what the Holy Spirit was to the prophets, so he was to the apostles; the authority of the one is equal to the authority of the other. In a similar way, in Revelation 22:6 John claimed that the God who controlled 'the spirits of the prophets' also revealed the contents of John's revelations to him.

If ever a church tested Paul's patience it must have been the church at Corinth; against no other church did he have to defend his apostolic authority so much. But it is useful for us that he had to do so. In 1 Corinthians 14:37 Paul made it quite clear that his words carried with them the authority of Jesus himself: 'If anybody thinks he is a prophet or spiritually gifted, let him acknowledge that what I am writing to you is the Lord's command.' Similarly, the apostle could remind the Thessalonians: 'You know what instructions we gave you by *the authority* of the Lord Jesus' (1 Thessalonians 4:2). The words in italics are not part of the original Greek, and have been unnecessarily added by some translators. Earlier in that same letter Paul reminded his readers how they had first responded to Paul's message: 'When you received the word of God, which you heard from us, you accepted it not as the word of men, but as it actually is, the word of God...' (2:13).

Because Paul was convinced that his teaching carried with it the authority of God, he was not reluctant to claim that his preaching was the standard of the truth and that other preachers could be tested and measured by it. In Galatians 1:6–12, Paul claimed that anyone preaching contrary to his teaching, even he himself if he ever dared to change the content of his gospel, should be cut off from God. The reason is, that Paul's gospel was not 'something that man made up', but was received 'by revelation from Jesus Christ' (vs 11–12). This chapter in Galatians must convince even the most casual reader that Paul saw the gospel that he preached as God-given, and not something of his own invention. It was precisely to insist on this point that Paul was writing to the Galatians.

For this reason, obedience to the apostle's teaching became a condition of fellowship:

'If anybody thinks he is a prophet or spiritually gifted, let him acknowledge that what I am writing to you is the Lord's command. If he ignores this, he himself will be ignored' (1 Corinthians 14:37–38).

'In the name of the Lord Jesus Christ, we command you, brothers, to keep away from every brother who is idle and does not live according to the teaching you received from us... If anyone does not obey our instruction in this letter, take special note of him. Do not associate with him, in order that he may feel ashamed' (2 Thessalonians 3:6, 14).

It cannot be suggested that Paul was claiming only that his general message, rather than the specific words, was given by the Holy Spirit. For a Jew and Pharisee with a high view of the Hebrew Scriptures, there was no such distinction. Every word was considered to be revealed by God and this explains the scribes' exhaustive care when copying the texts; not a single word or stroke of the pen (a 'jot or tittle') would be deliberately altered. For the scribal care in copying the texts see in this series Book 1 chapter 6 and Book 4 chapter 2.

For the apostles, inspiration—in the sense of the correct meaning of 'God-breathed'—was the same as revelation. Paul makes this clear in Ephesians 3 where he insists that his message was 'made known to me by revelation' (v 3) and 'revealed by the Spirit to God's holy apostles and prophets' (v 5). Whether the 'prophets' here are the Old or New Testament prophets is a matter of debate; either way, the apostles and prophets have the authority of God-given revelation through the Holy Spirit.

There are a few phrases used by Paul that may appear to present a challenge to the apostles' conviction that they spoke with the authority of God. When the apostle claimed in 1 Corinthians 7:10 that, 'I give this command (not I, but the Lord)' he meant that on the particular subject he is dealing with, Jesus had already spoken during his earthly ministry—see for example Matthew 19:1–9. On the other hand, when Paul declared in verse 12, 'To the rest I say this (I, not the Lord)' he meant that on this part of the subject Jesus had nothing directly to say. In this way we can understand verse 25 also. The phrase: 'I think that I too have the Spirit of God', found in verse 40, is not a statement of doubt. Paul is either making a sarcastic jibe at those in Corinth who claimed to be full of spiritual gifts and wisdom (they are found in 14:37), or else he is simply making a positive statement in much the same way that we might affirm the truth of a statement with the positive claim: 'I think I know what I am talking about.'

HOW THEIR LETTERS WERE TO BE RECEIVED

We have already noted that obedience to the letters of the apostles was a condition of fellowship in the churches; in addition to this, Paul did not expect his letters to be read once and then destroyed. The letter addressed to the Colossian church was to be read and then passed on to the church at Laodicea; similarly, the letter he had written to Laodicea, though this one has not come down to us, was to be read at Colossae (Colossians 4:16). The apostle was so insistent that his letter to the Thessalonian church should be read by everyone that he placed them under an obligation to the Lord himself to make sure that 'all the brothers' had it read to them (1 Thessalonians 5:27). There is a particular blessing promised to those who read and obey the words of John's Revelation (Revelation 1:3).

THE WORDS OF JESUS EQUAL WITH THE OLD TESTAMENT

Paul gave the words of Christ recorded in the Gospels equal authority with the Old Testament. In 1 Timothy 5:18 he was arguing that proper support should be given to those who lead, preach and teach in the church. To add scriptural authority to his command, the apostle quoted first from Deuteronomy 25:4, 'Do not muzzle an ox while it is treading out the grain' and then he quoted a phrase that is found only in Luke 10:7, 'The worker deserves his wages.' What is important here is the fact that in 1 Timothy 5:18 Paul introduced both quotations with the statement: 'The Scripture says…' Paul recognized the words of Jesus in Luke's Gospel as Scripture equally with the words of Moses in Deuteronomy. It is evident also that when Paul was dealing with the same subject in 1 Corinthians 9:9,14 he had these two quotations in his mind.

THE LETTERS OF THE APOSTLES AS SCRIPTURE

Peter gave Paul's letters the same authority as the Old Testament Scriptures. Most readers have sympathy with Peter's admission that some things in Paul's letters are 'hard to understand' (2 Peter 3:16). However, when Peter continued, 'which ignorant and unstable people distort, as they do the other Scriptures', it is clear that Peter considered Paul's letters carried the same authority as the Old Testament Scriptures and could therefore rightly be called 'the Scriptures'. Therefore, when we refer the 'all Scripture' in 2 Timothy 3:16 to both Old and New Testaments, we are only doing what the apostles themselves had begun to do even before the close of the New Testament.

THE AUTHORITY JESUS GAVE TO HIS DISCIPLES

The passage in Matthew 16:18–19 has often been the cause of debate and argument, but there is a particular phrase in verse 19 (found also in Matthew 18:18) that is relevant for our present subject:

'I will give you the keys of the kingdom of heaven; whatever you bind on earth will be bound in heaven, and whatever you loose on earth will be loosed in heaven.'

The Jewish background to this verse overcomes any difficulty of interpretation. The binding and loosing referred to, do not directly refer to the forgiveness of sins. That is referred to in John 20:23, but not here. The scribes of Israel were thought of as stewards of the treasures of divine wisdom (see for instance, Matthew 13:52) and when admitted to this office a scribe symbolically received the key of knowledge (there is a reference to this in Luke 11:52). The duty of the scribe (who, because of his knowledge of the Law of God was in effect a lawyer) was to interpret the Law of God to particular cases. He would inform a man whether a certain law applied to him or not. Therefore, when the scribes bound a man they placed him under the obligation of the Scriptures and he was prohibited from doing something; when they loosed him, they released him from the obligation. Similarly, the scribes claimed the authority to declare a man guilty (bound) or absolved (free).[50]

Jesus had been training his disciples to be stewards of the treasure of the new covenant—the gospel. In this promise in Matthew 16:19, he is referring to their future writing and preaching and effectively assuring them that they would have the authority of God's Law. In this sense they will be the true scribes of the new covenant, and to this end, Jesus promised his disciples special help in writing the New Testament. In John 14:26 he gave his disciples two promises—one was a divinely aided understanding, and the other was a divinely aided memory:

---

50 Alfred Edersheim, *The Life and Times of Jesus the Messiah*. 1883. (Pickering & Inglis Ltd, London 1959), Vol. 2, p. 645. See also William Hendriksen, *Gospel of Matthew* (Banner of Truth Trust, Edinburgh 1982), p. 651.

'The Counsellor, the Holy Spirit, whom the Father will send in my name, will teach you all things and will remind you of everything I have said to you.'

John 16:13 adds to this a divinely aided knowledge: 'He will tell you what is yet to come.'

Therefore, in order that the disciples might recall accurately all that Christ had said and done, instruct the Christian church in the way of truth, and write of things still in the future, Jesus promised the help of the Holy Spirit. The apostles would be writing with no less authority than the Old Testament prophets. This is confirmed in Revelation 22:6, 'The angel said to me, "These words are trustworthy and true. The Lord, the God of the spirits of the prophets, sent his angel to show his servants the things that must soon take place."'

The authority of Jesus himself

It may appear unnecessary to show that Jesus claimed to speak with the authority of God; we have only to demonstrate that he was the Son of God, equal with the Father and came from God and it follows that he spoke with divine authority. However, in several ways his authority was underlined throughout his ministry.

Jesus always saw his own teaching as holding a position of authority in some senses even greater than that of the Old Testament prophets. His declaration in his great prayer to his Father: 'I gave them the words you gave me...' (John 17:8) reflects the claims of the prophet; however, his repeated use of the phrase: 'I tell you'—over sixty times in Matthew's Gospel alone—cannot be matched by any of the prophets, who declared, 'This is what the LORD says.' For the prophets, their only authority was that of the word from God they were passing on; for Jesus the Messiah, he spoke on his own authority whilst acknowledging that this was in full agreement with his Father. On the Mount of Transfiguration the voice of God the Father gave approval to his Son's teaching with the words: 'This is my Son, whom I have chosen; listen to him' (Luke 9:35).

Nowhere did Christ more plainly express the authority of his teaching—an authority that would remain until heaven and earth pass away—than in Matthew 5:18, 'I tell you the truth, until heaven and earth disappear, not the smallest letter, not the least stroke of a pen, will by any means disappear from the Law until everything is accomplished.' Later in his ministry Jesus applied the same authority to his own words: 'Heaven and earth will pass away, but my words will never pass away' (Matthew 24:35).

The title of Christ as the *logos* ('Word' John 1:1–18) was intended to express the fact that not only his life was a revelation of God, but his spoken words carried the direct authority of the voice of God. For both the Jewish Pharisees and the Greek philosophers, John knew that the word *logos* carried with it the concept of the controlling 'voice' or power behind the universe. The Jews immediately thought of the creative word of God in Genesis 1:3, and the Greeks thought of the logos as the 'creative and controlling mind of God'.[51]

The prophetic office of Jesus Christ was like no other prophet. Moses told of a prophet who would come and who must be listened to (Deuteronomy 18:15); since many God-ordained prophets would follow Moses over the course of 1,500 years, the reference by Moses to a future prophet (singular), must refer to someone unique. Subsequently, God restated the importance of this prophet:

'I will raise up for them a prophet like you from among their brothers; I will put my words in his mouth, and he will tell them everything I command him. If anyone does not listen to my words that the prophet speaks in my name, I myself will call him to account' (Deuteronomy 18:18–19).

That this refers to the Messiah is clear from the application of the passage by Peter (Acts 3:22) and Stephen (Acts 7:37). They both used the passage in such a way that they assumed their hearers not only understood it, but acknowledged its Messianic reference. Evidently Philip also had this passage in mind when he introduced Nathaniel to Jesus: 'We have found the one Moses wrote about in the Law, and about whom the prophets also

---

51 This theme is discussed in detail by James Montgomery Boice, *The Gospel of John* (Zondervan, Grand Rapids 1975), Vol. 1, pp. 37–42.

wrote' (John 1:45). Similarly, John 6:14 shows that the people expected a specific Prophet to come as the Messiah: 'Surely this is the Prophet who is to come into the world.'

Since the Samaritans used only the Pentateuch (Genesis to Deuteronomy) as their Scriptures, it could only be the promise in Deuteronomy that the woman at the well had in mind when she asserted, 'I know that Messiah… is coming. When he comes, he will explain everything to us.' (John 4:25). She quoted Deuteronomy 18:18 virtually verbatim. There can be little doubt that Jesus had the same passage in mind when he challenged the Pharisees: 'If you believed Moses, you would believe me, for he wrote about me' (John 5:46).

In spite of, and perhaps because of, all this, modern Jewish interpretations consider the reference in Deuteronomy to be a collective noun for all the prophets—although the Hebrew word *nabi* (prophet) in the singular is never used of a collective noun; a few of the early church Fathers (Origen for example), took the same view. Others (including Calvin and Keil and Delitzsch), steered a middle course and believed it had reference to all the prophets culminating in the unique ministry of Jesus Christ. However, the most common view of the Reformed Christian churches has been that it refers uniquely to the Messiah, Jesus. This was certainly the position of most of the church Fathers and Luther. Significantly, against the modern Jewish interpretation, the older Jewish commentators prior to the birth of Jesus, almost all saw this passage as a promise of the coming Messiah.[52]

A reader may conclude that the writers of the Bible, both in the Old and New Testaments, were mistaken in their claim to an authority that came from God and that their words were the very words of God, but what can never be doubted is that this is exactly what they believed. This conviction runs consistently throughout the pages of the Bible and is believed by every writer and accepted by each for the others.

---

52 Ernst W Hengstenberg, *Christology of the Old Testament* Orig.1829–35. Trans.1854. (MacDonald Publishing Co, McLean, Virginia), Vol. 1, pp. 71–80.

6. Is the Bible enough?

Christians believe that the Bible is the final written revelation from God, and is sufficient for the church in every age. What does this mean? And what is the evidence for it?

When the General Assembly of the Church of Scotland met on 27 August 1647 it approved what is known as the *Westminster Confession of Faith*. This was a detailed statement of Christian belief governing the Presbyterian churches, and it began by affirming the authority and sufficiency of Scripture.

'The whole counsel of God, concerning all things necessary for His own glory, man's salvation, faith, and life, is either expressly set down in Scripture, or by good and necessary consequence may be deduced from Scripture: unto which nothing at any time is to be added, whether by new revelations of the Spirit, or by traditions of men.'[53]

The Baptist Confession of 1689 used almost identical language to describe the Baptist belief in the finality and sufficiency of Scripture.[54] Both agree that in our Bible we have God's word covering every area of what we believe about God and salvation and how we should live—either by direct statements or by principles—and that it should not be added to by any other authority, whether claiming to be from God or men.

So far, we have shown that the Bible demands that it is accepted as God's word with God's authority, and that it is completely reliable in all its statements, whether they involve doctrine, history, geography or practical Christian living. The question we must now answer is this: 'Is the Bible sufficient? Is it all we that we need to guide us in life? Is it enough?'

---

53 The *Westminster Confession of Faith* 1647, 1:6.
54 *The Baptist Confession of Faith* 1689, 1:6.

A definition of 'sufficient and final'

When we speak of the sufficiency and finality of Scripture we mean that in the Bible, the human race in every century and in every culture, has everything that God wants to tell us *infallibly* about everything. In matters of what God expects us to believe about the Christian faith and how God expects us to live, we do not need any more.

There are two parts to this definition:

First, there are things we may want to know—and we can certainly discover more as the story of man's thinking, invention and exploration develops—but God will not give us any more Scripture ('everything that God wanted to tell us *infallibly*') on any subject. We have all the infallibly given words from God needed for any subject.

The second part of our definition affirms that on issues of what we believe about the Christian faith (Christian doctrine and practice), whilst there is more we may want to know, there is nothing else that we need to know and nothing else that we can know that is wholly reliable.

Nothing in this definition of sufficiency discourages the enquiring mind and relentless discovery of the natural world. However, in matters of doctrine and behaviour there are many things that we would like to know, but there is nothing more that we can know beyond that which is revealed in the Bible; we must not go beyond what is written (1 Corinthians 4:6). There are always 'secret things' that belong to God alone (Deuteronomy 29:29). On the door of heaven hangs a notice that reads: 'Enquire within'.

This does not preclude the value of excellent books, commentaries, sermons and teaching that explain the Scriptures, but none of this carries the same God-given authority as the Bible itself. In Nehemiah 8:8 the Levites: 'Read from the book of the Law of God, making it clear and giving the meaning, so that the people could understand what was being read.' The words of the Levites were wise and helpful, but not infallible. In contrast to God's revelation in the Bible, all other views of God and the human race and salvation are unreliable. Similarly, the Bible contains all that we need to know about how to live to please God. No other words can speak to us with the same authority and completeness, and there can never be any more words from God added to the Bible.

Does the Bible teach sufficiency and finality?

Paul claimed that 'all Scripture is God-breathed and is useful for teaching, rebuking, correcting and training in righteousness, so that the man of God may be thoroughly equipped for every good work' (2 Timothy 3:16–17). The words 'thoroughly equipped' translate one small Greek word (*artios*) which means 'complete'. In other words, the Scriptures can make a Christian 'complete' for the service of God. The picture is that of the soldier fully equipped with all that he needs for battle. The Scriptures are therefore sufficient and nothing else is required. It is in this context that the word *theopneustos* (God-breathed) is used. See chapter 2 in this book for a discussion of 'God-breathed'. In the mind of the apostles, no other writing than the Scriptures, carries the finality of divine revelation.

When Jesus promised the disciples that his Holy Spirit would guide them into 'all truth' (John 16:13), it was a promise that they would be given infallible aid in the writing of Scripture. A more accurate translation of what our Lord said to his disciples would be: 'But when he comes, the Spirit of truth, he will guide you *in all the truth*.' In other words, not only would all that they wrote be truth, but all that they wrote would be all the truth that would be given on the subject of the life of Christ. God may give his people more light on the truth in later generations of the church, but he will not give them any more truth. They have all that they need.

When Paul wrote to the Corinthians, he had experienced some difficulty with that church's attitude to his authority as an apostle. In the course of explaining that he was secure in his apostleship, whether or not they judged him correctly, Paul reminded them of the expression: 'Do not go beyond what is written' (1 Corinthians 4:6). Although we are not aware of any wording quite like this elsewhere, evidently Paul and his readers were; and the phrase 'what is written' is a common enough way in which Paul referred to the Old Testament Scriptures; he uses it sixteen times in his letter to the Romans alone, and more than thirty times in all. Therefore, as

Chapter 6

Leon Morris concludes, 'We may fairly conjecture that "Not beyond what is written" was a catchphrase familiar to Paul and his readers, directing attention to the need for conformity to Scripture.'[55] We may rightly add, and to Scripture alone.

In a similar way, Jude 3 encouraged the Christians to 'contend for the faith that was *once for all* entrusted to the saints.' Clearly, Jude had in mind the fact that the content of the Christian gospel had been finally given through the apostles, and nothing more could be added. Significantly, the same word translated 'once for all' is used in Hebrews 9:28 with reference to the death of Christ for sin.

An interesting warning appears three times in Scripture. It is found in Deuteronomy 4:2 (repeated in 12:32), in Proverbs 30:6 and finally in Revelation 22:18–19. In the first, God warns: 'Do not add to what I command you and do not subtract from it.' In the second, we are told: 'Do not add to his words, or he will rebuke you and prove you a liar.' In the third, a severe judgement is threatened on those who either add to or take away from, anything in the prophecies of the book of Revelation. It may be suggested that these warnings have to do only with the books of the Bible in which they are found, however, clearly God has placed these three passages at three strategic places in the history of his people as a constant reminder that nothing can be added to his infallible verbal revelation.

THE SCRIPTURES SPEAK WITH FINALITY

Much of the support for the Bible as sufficient is found by inference rather than a plain statement. The New Testament always implies its finality, and nowhere promises further revelation that will carry the same God-breathed authority.

When Paul wrote to Timothy, he encouraged the young pastor at Ephesus to: 'Guard what has been entrusted to your care' (1 Timothy 6:20), and Peter, in words that implied a finality, similarly encouraged the churches to remember his teaching—as if the importance was that there would be no more to follow when the apostles have gone:

55 Leon Morris, *The First Epistle of Paul to the Corinthians* (Tyndale Press, London 1958), p. 78.

'I will always remind you of these things, even though you know them and are firmly established in the truth you now have. I think it is right to refresh your memory as long as I live in the tent of this body, because I know that I will soon put it aside, as our Lord Jesus Christ has made clear to me. And I will make every effort to see that after my departure you will always be able to remember these things' (2 Peter 1:12–15).

Jude implied the same: 'But, dear friends, remember what the apostles of our Lord Jesus Christ foretold' (Jude 17). There is an urgency in the New Testament letters for the churches to keep and remember what they have been taught because there is nothing more to come.

When Jesus was speaking to his disciples in John 14–16, some of what he promised was especially for them, and we cannot apply it to every Christian in every age. When he promised the apostles that the Holy Spirit would 'teach you all things and will remind you of everything I have said to you' (John 14:26). He did not limit the 'all things' to things necessary only for the first hundred years of the church. He meant all things necessary for his people in all ages. Similarly, in John 16:13–15 he promised the apostles that his Spirit would give to them all the truth necessary for the church for ever. This is not simply doctrinal truth, but practical truth also.

Because of this, Paul could remind the Ephesian Christians that the church is built upon the teaching of 'the apostles and prophets, with Christ Jesus himself as the chief cornerstone' (Ephesians 2:20). Once again there is a finality here; no one else is mentioned as part of this foundation. There will be no more apostles and no more prophets, just as Christ is the only cornerstone.

There is an interesting development through the New Testament which must be significant. As it progresses, less and less reference is made to prophets and prophecy, and more and more emphasis is placed upon preaching and teaching. In fact, the only references to New Testament prophecy in the letters are found in 1 Corinthians 12–14, three times in Ephesians, where Paul says it is foundational, and one each in Romans, Thessalonians and in 1 Timothy (where it refers to something that happened thirteen years earlier).

However, when Paul gave his final instructions to Timothy he urged him to pay attention to 'the public reading of Scripture, to preaching and teaching' (1 Timothy 4:13) and to 'preach the word' (2 Timothy 4:2). Similarly, the elders whose work is 'preaching and teaching' are worthy of double honour (1 Timothy 5:17).

In 2 Peter 2:1, Peter compared the false *prophets* in the Old Testament with the false *teachers* in his own day. The New Testament letters have much to say about teaching and preaching, but they have very little to say about prophecy and revelations. The reason is surely clear: God's plan for his church was changing as he brought his verbal revelation to a close and continued to lead his church through the faithful teaching of what he had already said. In other words, as the New Testament progresses there is a clear shift from revelation to proclamation, from prophets to teachers. This does not prohibit all prophecy, but significantly alters the balance.

THE SCRIPTURES CONDEMN THE TRADITIONS OF MEN
In the time of Christ, the Jews had gathered a great amount of teaching from their Rabbis; this was often placed alongside Scripture and almost given the same authority as Scripture itself. Much of this teaching was nonsense, although some of it was good and profitable (see chapter 3 in this book). However, Jesus never allowed any of it to stand beside Scripture, and he warned the Pharisees against it: 'Why do you break the command of God for the sake of your tradition?' (Matthew 15:3). Reminding them of Isaiah 29, he accused the Jewish leaders: 'You nullify the word of God by your tradition' (Mark 7:13). This warning against tradition should be enough to avoid any addition to the Scriptures.

QUALIFICATIONS FOR THOSE WHO CLAIM TO GIVE THE WORD OF GOD
It has long been accepted that all who gave us the New Testament Scriptures were qualified in a way that is not possible for anyone of a later age. When the eleven apostles were looking for someone to take the place of Judas Iscariot there were two essential qualifications they demanded: first, he must be a man who had been in company with Christ throughout the three years of his ministry and second, he must have

seen Jesus after the resurrection (Acts 1:21–22). It was from men who fulfilled these conditions that, either directly or indirectly, the whole of our New Testament came. See Book 3 chapter 6 of this series: 'Who wrote the books of the New Testament?' Paul was an unusual apostle, as he himself admitted in 1 Corinthians 15:8–9, and he had to defend his right to speak and write as an apostle against those who doubted that he had really seen Christ (see 1 Corinthians 9:1–2). Both Peter (2 Peter 1:16–18) and John (1 John 1:1–3) emphasized their qualification of having lived with Jesus and witnessed his resurrection. No one can fulfil these conditions today.

How sufficient is sufficient?

SUFFICIENT FOR EVERYTHING?

To say the Bible is sufficient may tell us very little because we then need to ask, 'Sufficient for what?' If we imply that the Bible tells us all we need to know about everything, then we at once put a stop to all scientific research and we cease asking questions about anything not directly mentioned in the Bible. But the Bible is relevant, not ridiculous. God has given us minds and skills, and both are to be used to benefit humanity. Job speaks of man's enquiring mind and his amazing discoveries and achievements (see especially Job 28) and nowhere does God even hint that these things are wrong. It is the genius of the human race—like nothing in the animal kingdom—to learn, discover and invent.

Clearly there are many subjects upon which the Bible is silent; for example, it has nothing to say directly about the technical problems of space travel or the control of dangerous viruses and bacteria whether in our bodies or computers, and scientists are not wrong to study these subjects.

On the other hand, if we say the Bible is sufficient in the subjects about which it does speak, have we really helped very much? After all, the Bible does say something about business dealings (see, for example, James 4:13–15), building construction (Matthew 7:24–27; Luke 14:28), farming (2 Timothy 2:6) and shepherding (John 10), but no one would claim that it says everything there is to be said about these activities. Sufficiency does not mean that the Bible is all we need to know about everything. We said earlier that in the Bible we do not have everything we need to know or want to know about everything, but we have everything that God *infallibly* tells us about everything.

SUFFICIENT FOR THE MAIN PURPOSE

What is the purpose of the Bible? If its chief purpose was to be a complete handbook for the space engineer or the micro-biologist, the business salesman or the building contractor, the farmer or the shepherd, then we would expect it to say everything and could rightly criticize it for anything it left out. In fact, the Bible is first of all a book about God. It tells us infallibly all we need to know, and all we shall ever need to know on earth, about God: who he is, what he is like, what he does and, of course, how we can know him. In this area it is sufficient; it is enough.

The Bible is also a book about the human race and salvation. It tells us accurately how the human race began, and in detail what we are like; not physically, because our bodies are only a part of us. It tells us especially about our real selves, our souls. It tells us how and why we have gone wrong, and how things can be put right. This is detailed in The Master Plan in Book 1 chapter 1 of this series. On these subjects the Bible is sufficient because it leaves nothing for us to guess or make up that we *need* to know. In this area, God cannot leave us to discover the answers for ourselves. Because our minds and souls are so marred by sin, human knowledge and wisdom will never find God. Paul reminds us of this, 'The world, through its wisdom, did not know him' (1 Corinthians 1:21). In fact, as Paul makes clear, although men and women should be able to know God through the revelation of creation, in reality: 'they neither glorified him as God nor gave thanks to him, but their thinking became futile and their foolish hearts were darkened' (Romans 1:21).

Therefore, on the subject of doctrine (theology)—what we should believe about God, the human race and salvation—the Bible leaves no areas unclear that we need to know about. There are many things that the Bible has not revealed even in these areas, and we must therefore conclude that we do not need to know about them. On the subject of doctrine, the Bible is both clear and sufficient; it is enough.

SUFFICIENT PRINCIPLES

In an age of moral confusion over the value of life, marriage, sexuality, gender and a host of other vital issues, the Bible does not simply present principles, but provides mandates for holy as opposed to promiscuous or immoral living. Many such issues are spelt out clearly throughout the Bible and it is only wilful disobedience that fails to see it. These areas of practical morality are clearly set out in the Bible to reveal God's plan for the good order of individual and social life. The Bible does not say everything that could be said, but it says everything that needs to be said from God for us to know just how we should govern our lives. As a handbook for Christian morality and citizenship the Bible is sufficient, it is enough.

However, where there are not specific statements to govern a particular situation, there are general statements (principles) that we can apply. These principles will be found in the Scriptures and can be worked out in many different circumstances.

In the world of medicine there is a principle that sterilization kills germs and prevents infection; that is the general statement or principle, but how we actually apply that principle will differ according to the situation. A dressing or a surgical knife can be steam-sterilized at a temperature of 120° Centigrade, but a different method is needed to sterilize a dirty wound! However, we can rightly claim that the principle of sterilizing to avoid infection is sufficient. In the same way when Jesus was asked whether or not it was right to pay taxes to a pagan ruler, his answer: 'Give to Caesar what is Caesar's, and to God what is God's' (Matthew 22:21), dealt not merely with that particular question but provided a principle that can be applied in many other situations.

The Christian does not dare to live without constant reference to the Bible, because, whilst the standards and principles of the world are always shifting, those of the Bible never change. Here, in the Bible, are commands and principles that are both sufficient and completely reliable for all Christians in every age and culture.

A belief in the sufficiency of the Bible both for doctrine and for living—for what we believe and how we live—does not mean that we have an answer to every issue that confronts us. A frequent challenge to the Christian is, 'What happens to an infant who dies before reaching an age when it could reasonably be expected to respond to God's offer of salvation, or to those who live with a significantly impaired mental development?' Many Christians immediately conclude, 'It goes to heaven, of course.' However, nowhere in the Bible are we explicitly told this; that response also begs the question of what age 'infants' are responsible for their own commitment.[56] There are indications perhaps, but the Bible is silent on this subject; it is one of those secrets not revealed to us. Lacking a clear statement from Scripture we do not guess or make up an answer, but we look for a principle that will guide us; and we find one in Genesis 18:25, 'Will not the Judge of all the earth do right?' That must settle it. We do not know for certain what happens to the infant who dies, or the child cruelly aborted in the womb, or those born with a mind incapable of reasoning, but we do know that God is just and right in all that he does and we can safely leave the problem there.

Paul himself provides a helpful example of the value of looking for the principles found in Scripture. In 1 Timothy 5:17 it is his intention to encourage the churches to support those who lead the work and are 'full-time' in Christian service, but where will he find support for this in the Old Testament? Paul turned to Deuteronomy 25:4, 'Do not muzzle an ox while it is treading out the grain.' The apostle drew on this principle that if an ox is being used to turn the mill stone or drag the threshing sledge, he should at least benefit from his work by being allowed to eat the grain. Paul obviously enjoyed this principle because in 1 Corinthians 9:8–12 he elaborated and went so far as to say that this particular law was not written primarily for kindness to oxen, but for us:

---

56 David's response to the death of his young son in 2 Samuel 12:23 'Can I bring him back again? I will go to him, but he will not return to me', is sometimes used in this connection, but it is not conclusive. It is unwise to make a theology out of the heart-cry of a grieving father.

'Doesn't the Law say the same thing? For it is written in the Law of Moses: "Do not muzzle an ox while it is treading out the grain." Is it about oxen that God is concerned? Surely he says this for us, doesn't he? Yes, this was written for us, because when the ploughman ploughs and the thresher threshes, they ought to do so in the hope of sharing in the harvest. If we have sown spiritual seed among you, is it too much if we reap a material harvest from you? If others have this right of support from you, shouldn't we have it all the more?'

On this basis, the Old Testament is full of principles for a modern world. See for example Deuteronomy 22:6 (ecology), v.8 (health and safety), v.10 (animal welfare). The Scripture is therefore sufficient not only on matters of doctrine, but also for practical Christian living, because there are principles in Scripture that will guide us in any and every situation.

Why do we differ?

There are some subjects on which God has spoken, but not in a way that is so clear as to avoid differences among Christians. There are many things we do in our churches that have no direct scriptural support and there are many areas of understanding the Bible where Christians, equally committed to the full inspiration and authority of Scripture, are in fairly radical disagreement. In the light of this can we still hold to the sufficiency of Scripture? If it is sufficient, why do we not all agree about everything? There are two answers to this.

In the first place, even the Christian has a mind that has been heavily influenced by culture, tradition and sin. As a result, we often impose on the Bible our own understanding of what it is saying. We all come to the Bible with our traditions, prejudices and preferences and that affects how we understand it. The fault lies in us, not in the Bible. In the same way, we must humbly admit that our fallen mind cannot always grasp the deep things about God that are revealed in the Bible; there will be some things that, although revealed to us, are beyond our ability fully to understand. Given these limitations we should be grateful that nevertheless God has given us a complete Bible. How much confusion would result if the Bible was still an unfinished book is evidenced by the strange and contradictory views of those who do add to the Bible!

The second answer is that although God has told us clearly what we need to know, there are many details he allows us to work out according to the conditions of our local situation. We must always distinguish between something that is contrary to Scripture and something that is not in Scripture: a thing may be non-scriptural without being against Scripture. We are allowed to do things not specifically mentioned in Scripture provided they are not contrary to Scripture; that is, provided they are in harmony with scriptural principles.

Some Christians talk about 'the regulative principle'. This is an expression which means that the Scriptures must regulate or control all that we do in our own lives and in our churches. This is true, but the phrase, 'the regulative principle', must never be taken to mean that we cannot do something unless we can find a specific mention of it in the Bible. The writer to the Hebrews resolved this for us. In Hebrews 5:14 he encouraged his readers: 'Solid food is for the mature, who by constant use have trained themselves to distinguish good from evil.' We may ask, 'constant use of what?' The answer is found in the previous verse, where the writer refers to 'the teaching about righteousness'. In other words, the Christian must learn to use the Bible as the source book from which principles will be found that speak to us in every area of life and faith.

If we take an example from the area of organizing the local church we can see this difference between things that are legitimate, but not specifically mentioned in Scripture, and those that are clearly against the principles of Scripture. A church may keep a formal list or register of those who are members of the church. Nowhere is this practice explicitly found in Scripture, but in order to follow the principle of doing things properly and in an orderly manner (1 Corinthians 14:40), and to know who is committed to the church and who is allowed to help make important decisions, they may decide that it is a sensible and practical idea. It is not contrary to Scripture in that there is nothing in Scripture that says or implies that such a practice is wrong, and in fact the implication is the other way: how else could troublemakers and heretics be cast out of the church (1 Corinthians 5:13) unless the church knew who belonged in the first place?

On the other hand, suppose the church then decides to make a charge for membership amounting to one week's pay each month. The Scripture gives us clear principles to guide our giving, and these include the fact that for the Christian, giving should be freely, joyfully and willingly from the heart. Paul's principles in 1 Corinthians 16:1–2 and 2 Corinthians 8:2–5; 9:6–13 for example, are clearly against any such 'membership fee'. We can therefore conclude that such a compulsory 'charge' to members is not merely non-scriptural but against Scripture; it is against the principles laid down in Scripture.

This is a very important distinction. We can still see that even in these areas, Scripture is sufficient; it is our guide as to whether or not something should be done. It is sufficient to tell us whether we *must* do something, whether we *may* do it, or whether we *must not* do it.

A summary of sufficiency

The sufficiency of Scripture does not mean that Scripture says everything we need to know on every subject. However, it does mean that Scripture says everything we need to know on the chief subjects of the Bible, such as what we should believe about God, the human race and salvation. In all other areas, such as living the Christian life in a modern world, or organizing a local church, Scripture gives us clear mandates on some issues and clear principles on others. These are sufficient to guide us in any and every situation. Whatever subject it speaks about, the Bible gives us all the infallible revelation from God that we need.

On any issue, we must ask ourselves: 'Is my proposed action clearly against Scripture or simply not in Scripture?' If it is the latter, then we look for principles to govern that course of action. In every case, Scripture is sufficient. All matters of doctrine and life are to be brought to the final test of Scripture. There are no subjects upon which it has nothing to say either by direct command or indirect principle.

The Bible is also sufficient to help us understand its own message. Valuable as books and commentaries may be, they are not essential to a correct understanding of the Bible. A humble and spiritually wise mind, by reading thoughtfully and comparing Scripture with Scripture, is quite capable of understanding its message and applying it relevantly to life.

The alternative to sufficient and final

If the Bible is not sufficient and final, then confusion results. This is surely why, as the New Testament progresses, there is a clear shift from revelation to proclamation. God knew exactly what would happen if his church was allowed to add new prophecies to its life and work.

We would expect God to make his word clear and final and not to leave us to the illusions of imagination, enthusiasm or the majority vote of contemporary culture. No military officer would give an order that invites others to add to it as they pass it down the line of command; the result would be confusion.

The converted eighteenth century slave trader, John Newton, wrote of the assistance the Holy Spirit gives as we read the Scriptures:

'We are directed to expect the teaching and assistance of the Holy Spirit only within the limits, and by the medium of the written word. He has not promised to reveal new truths, but to enable us to understand what we read in the Bible; and if we venture beyond the pale of Scripture, we are upon enchanted ground, and exposed to all the illusions of imagination and enthusiasm. But an attention to the word of God, joined to humble supplications for his Spirit, will lead us to new advances in true knowledge.'[57]

THE ROMAN CATHOLIC VIEW

Alongside the Bible, the Roman Catholic church has placed a number of human traditions; this includes most of the *Apocrypha* (which they call 'deutero-canonical'. See Book 3 chapter 2 in this series for the *Apocrypha*), some of the writings of church leaders in the first few centuries, and a collection of decrees and statements given by popes and church councils

---

57 John Newton, 'Fourteen Letters to the Rev Dr Dixon, St Edmund Hall, Oxford, 6 September 1768.' Letters intended as a sequel to *Cardiphonia. The Works of John Newton* (Banner of Truth, Edinburgh 1985 orig. 1820), Vol. VI, p. 203.

down the centuries. In 1546 the Council of Trent declared that all this extra material is to be taken as equal in authority to the Bible. This is still the official position of the Roman Catholic Church, which therefore denies the sufficiency of the Bible alone.

Consequently, the Roman church is faced with serious and embarrassing contradictions among her popes, teachers and 'saints', each of whom has 'added' to Scripture. For thirty years towards the end of the fourteenth century there were two popes, one at Rome and the other at Avignon; each excommunicating the other and each claiming to be the true successor of Peter. For a year, there were even three popes. This, together with the contradictory teachings from the various schools of doctrine, denies the claim that Rome has added a consistent tradition to the Bible. The sixteenth century Protestant Reformers, like Martin Luther and John Calvin, had little difficulty in quoting 'Fathers' of the Roman church whose writings actually supported the Reformation theology and condemned current Roman teaching.

THE LIBERAL VIEW

If Catholicism adds to the sufficiency of Scripture, the liberal theologian, who denies both the accuracy and authority of the Bible, subtracts from it. The liberal approach to Scripture doubts that the Bible is reliable in its statements about history, and often denies the reality of miracles and other supernatural experiences, and declares virtually all Bible doctrine to be a matter of personal opinion that we may accept or reject.

Not all critics of the Bible are as extreme in their views as this, but some are much worse. To many, the Bible is largely irrelevant for the modern world, and it has little to say to help us with the issues of today. There is no agreement among them as to how much and what parts of the Bible we can accept. Millions of words and thousands of books have been produced over the last one hundred and fifty years by those who deny the Bible and its authority and sufficiency, but still the critics disagree among themselves about almost everything. That is confusion, not order.

THE VIEW OF THE CULTS

Almost all modern 'Christian' sects that have formed themselves into strong organizations have added to the Bible, although some would strongly disagree with this suggestion.

The Mormons (the Latter Day Saints of Jesus Christ) use the *Book of Mormon, Doctrines and Covenants* and *The Pearl of Great Price*, most of which were written by Joseph Smith and all are considered to be equal in authority with the Bible. However, there is significant controversy, even among Mormons, over the genuineness of some of these. In addition, they claim their international president can speak with infallibility, in much the same way as Roman Catholics believe the pope can when he is speaking as Peter's representative. To prove that the Bible prophesies the coming of the *Book of Mormon*, the Latter Day Saints refer to the two sticks in Ezekiel 37:15–23—the Bible and the *Book of Mormon*.

The Christian Science movement claims divine authority for *Science and Health* by Mary Baker Eddy and believe that this book is the 'little scroll' of Revelation 10:2 and that Mary Baker Eddy is the woman of Revelation 12.

Many, though not all, of the Christadelphians believe that *Elpis Israel* by John Thomas is the final understanding of the Bible and therefore the Bible is incomplete without it. This is certainly implied by Robert Roberts, a leading Christadelphian who, in 1874, claimed, 'To the charge of holding that the knowledge of the Scriptures in the writing of Dr Thomas has reached a finality, we plead guilty.'

Similarly, no teaching is allowed among the Jehovah's Witnesses without reference to the Governing Body of the Watchtower Society. In 1925 the London Convention of the Jehovah's Witnesses was ignored by the press, and the movement at once decided that London was the 'throne of the beast' referred to in Revelation 16:10. The movement has frequently changed its 'authoritative' position on many issues, including whether Jesus died on a stake or a cross (see in this series Book 1 chapter 4 'Was Jesus crucified?'), and when precisely was his 'second coming'.

Seventh Day Adventists believe that the teachings of their founder Ellen G White are essential to a proper understanding of Scripture and for many, observing the Saturday Sabbath is the only way to obtain salvation.

Such claims show that the cults do not believe the Bible to be sufficient in itself without the addition or aid of their own writings. It is therefore doubtful whether any of the cults really believes, or at least practises, the sufficiency of Scripture.

THE VIEW OF SOME 'CHARISMATIC' CHRISTIANS

In an attempt to emphasise the immanence of God (that is, God among us here and now), some 'charismatic' Christians suggest that whereas Scripture is God's 'horizontal' communication (words from the past), modern prophecy is a 'vertical' communication (words from God now). It is this dynamic value of prophecy today that they see as so valuable. They acknowledge that modern 'prophecy' is not an alternative, addition or advance on Scripture, because it is 'directional not doctrinal' and 'in all matters of faith and practice Scripture is both final and universal.' Nevertheless, they maintain that the need is for immediate as well as historic revelation, adding that whilst 'Scripture gives strategy, prophecy provides tactics.' Such prophecy, 'once its divine inspiration has been established, carries the same authority as scripture since both carry the authority of the same Lord who has spoken and is speaking. Both are to be obeyed.'[58]

Perhaps unintentionally, this denies the full sufficiency of Scripture because for them Scripture is not quite sufficient if the church requires more revelation from God for her normal life and growth. It also overlooks the Scriptures themselves as a dynamic revelation—or as the writer to the Hebrews expressed it: 'living and active' (4:12). The Bible is *both* horizontal and vertical revelation; it is God speaking to every generation through his word. To add prophecy as a necessary 'directional' aid is in danger of bypassing what the Bible refers to as a mature mind 'trained

---

58 J David Pawson in *Renewal* October 1990, pp.18–20 fairly represents this view of some charismatic Christians.

by constant practice to distinguish good from evil' (Hebrews 5:14); this 'constant practice', comes from 'the word of righteousness' which is the Bible. It also fails to acknowledge the shift noted earlier, as the New Testament develops, from prophecy to teaching (2 Peter 2:1).

One response to this 'charismatic' view has suggested that prophecy in the New Testament is not the same as Old Testament prophecy and therefore prophecies in the church today, because they do not carry the same authority, are valuable without conflicting with Scripture; they are little more than 'telling something that God has spontaneously brought to mind.' Assuming that there were 'prophets in the local congregations after the death of the apostles', this view concludes that they did not have authority equal to that of the apostles; they could be tested and they could be wrong.[59] This at least guards against adding anything significantly authoritative to Scripture, and could be understood as suggesting nothing more than what Christian have always believed: an idea that may or may not come from God.

However, there is little evidence for this popular conclusion that New Testament prophecy is significantly different from that in the Old Testament. As was noted earlier, the Catholic scholar, David Aune, in his treatment of the subject, though not responding to the issue of charismatic prophecy, demonstrated that in the first century the word 'prophet' was always used of 'One who speaks in place of or on behalf of the god',[60] and that in the New Testament the word is consciously borrowed 'from the widely accepted equation [equivalence] in Judaism of the Greek word *prophetes* with the Hebrew word *nabi*'.[61] David Aune argues that the New Testament apostles were the 'functional equivalent of the Old Testament prophet'.[62] There is no evidence that prophecy in the New Testament was ever anything less than this.

---

59 For example, Wayne A Grudem, 'Why Christians can still Prophesy', in *Christianity Today*, 16 September 1988, pp. 29–35.
60 David Aune, *Prophecy in Early Christianity and the Ancient Mediterranean World* (Eerdmans Publishing, Grand Rapids 1983), p. 29.
61 As above, p. 195.
62 As above, p. 202.

The only contrary evidence suggested is, first that the church was encouraged to test prophecy (2 Thessalonians 5:21), and second that the prophet Agabus was not quite correct in the details of the arrest of Paul in Jerusalem (compare Acts 21:10–11 with vv. 30–33).[63] However, even the prophets of the Old Testament were 'tested', otherwise how would a false prophet be discovered? As for Agabus, there is no discrepancy between his prophecy and the arrest of Paul; the slight differences in detail are easily understood as all part of the same violent events.

God reserves the right to reveal something significant to any of his servants at any time, and this may be in the form of a prophecy, but this does not imply the continuing presence of prophets in the church today. For those who believe that the Bible is sufficient and final, the church can be strong and healthy without any such revelations.

The importance of sufficiency and finality

It is not difficult to show that even among those who believe in the finality and sufficiency of Scripture, there have been and still are, significant divisions. Finality and sufficiency do not guarantee unity. There is always the danger of forgetting finality and sufficiency when the plain meaning of Scripture runs counter to our personal preference or traditions or to the culture of the day. An acceptance of gay and lesbian relationships by some who would profess to believe in sufficiency and finality can only be driven by the generally accepted view of society since the Bible could hardly be more transparent on the issue. Similarly, the re-interpretation of the early chapters of Genesis by others is driven only by the evolutionary mantra of contemporary geological theories. In each case the plain sense of Scripture is not sufficient.

However, for the most part, the differences among those who are committed to sufficiency and finality are more in the realm of what we believe about the church and its organization (ecclesiology). On the larger and more vital issues of theology—such as the Triune God, the nature and fall of the human race, the virgin conception, propitiatory

---

63 So Grudem as above.

death and literal resurrection of Jesus Christ, and the way of salvation by the new birth and faith alone—there is a huge area of total agreement between those who believe in the finality and sufficiency of the Bible. There is similarly wide agreement on issues of morality (what is right and wrong) and the value of human life. Confusion—tragic and unnecessary though it is—is generally at a much lower level of significant, but not vital, issues.

When we need to know the will of God for our own lives, a belief in the sufficiency of Scripture will direct us to find our answer from the statements and principles of God's final verbal revelation, and nowhere else; we must train ourselves to use God's word rather than to seek easy answers elsewhere. When we need to test the claims of the cults, Christian traditions, political correctness, or scientific theories, we shall know immediately where to go.

A belief in the sufficiency of Scripture is humbling, for it reminds us that there are some things we would like to know, but on which God has chosen not to give us an answer. There is a reverent agnosticism that does not try to invent a reasonable Christian response but recognizes that: 'The secret things belong to the Lord our God, but the things revealed belong to us and to our children for ever, that we may follow all the words of this law' (Deuteronomy 29:29).

Sufficiency means also that we must not add to Scripture nor take from it and that, as a consequence of this, we must never demand anything that is not found directly or by implication in Scripture—that would be Pharisaic legalism. But we should not expect less either. In other words, we must believe and live the true balance of Scripture.

Evangelical Christians throughout the history of the church, have believed firmly and from the teaching of Scripture itself, that with the close of the New Testament, God's inspired and infallible revelation came to an end. After the book of Malachi at the end of the Old Testament, God gave no more verbal revelation until the coming of Christ at his incarnation; in the same way, after the close of the New Testament God has no more verbal revelation until the coming of Christ in glory at the end of this age. The book we call the Bible is God's final word to the human race until Christ returns. It is the authoritative word of God and it is a sufficient guide for every aspect of Christian belief and practice.

7. The Chicago statement on biblical inerrancy

In 1977 the International Council on Biblical Inerrancy was formed in the United States of America under the chairmanship of James Montgomery Boice with a council of sixteen. Concerned at the erosion of a belief in the authority and accuracy of Scripture, the ICBI set out to provide conferences and publications that would explain the evangelical position on inerrancy. After ten years of vigorous work the council considered its work complete and the organization closed down.

From the start, the ICBI intended to be international and interdenominational in its representation. Membership of the council and forty-six strong advisory board included: Jay Adams, Edmund Clowney, Norman Geisler, Kenneth Kantzer, James Kennedy, John MacArthur, Roger Nicole, James Packer, Luis Palau and R C Sproul.

A statement on hermeneutics was also produced, but the following statement sets out the council's commitment to biblical inerrancy. As a clear and concise statement outlining the historic evangelical understanding of the authority and inerrancy of the Bible, it cannot be bettered. It repays a careful and thoughtful reading.

THE COUNCIL'S PREFACE

The authority of Scripture is a key issue for the Christian Church in this and every age. Those who profess faith in Jesus Christ as Lord and Saviour are called to show the reality of their discipleship by humbly and faithfully obeying God's written Word. To stray from Scripture in faith or conduct is disloyalty to our Master. Recognition of the total truth and trustworthiness of Holy Scripture is essential to a full grasp and adequate confession of its authority.

The following Statement affirms this inerrancy of Scripture afresh, making clear our understanding of it and warning against its denial. We are persuaded that to deny it is to set aside the witness of Jesus Christ and of the Holy Spirit and to refuse that submission to the claims of God's own Word which marks true Christian faith. We see it as our timely duty to make this affirmation in the face of current lapses from the truth of inerrancy among our fellow Christians and misunderstanding of this doctrine in the world at large.

This Statement consists of three parts: a Summary Statement, Articles of Affirmation and Denial, and an accompanying Exposition [the Exposition is not printed here]. It has been prepared in the course of a three-day consultation in Chicago. Those who have signed the Summary Statement and the Articles wish to affirm their own conviction as to the inerrancy of Scripture and to encourage and challenge one another and all Christians to a growing appreciation and understanding of this doctrine. We acknowledge the limitations of a document prepared in a brief, intensive conference and do not propose that this Statement be given creedal weight. Yet we rejoice in the deepening of our own convictions through our discussions together, and we pray that the Statement we have signed may be used to the glory of our God toward a new reformation of the Church in its faith, life, and mission.

We offer this Statement in a spirit, not of contention, but of humility and love, which we purpose by God's grace to maintain in any future dialogue arising out of what we have said. We gladly acknowledge that many who deny the inerrancy of Scripture do not display the consequences of this denial in the rest of their belief and behaviour, and we are conscious that we who confess this doctrine often deny it in life by failing to bring our thoughts and deeds, our traditions and habits, into true subjection to the divine Word.

We invite response to this statement from any who see reason to amend its affirmations about Scripture by the light of Scripture itself, under whose infallible authority we stand as we speak. We claim no personal infallibility for the witness we bear, and for any help which enables us to strengthen this testimony to God's Word we shall be grateful.

A SHORT STATEMENT

1. God, who is Himself Truth and speaks truth only, has inspired Holy Scripture in order thereby to reveal Himself to lost mankind through Jesus Christ as Creator and Lord, Redeemer and Judge. Holy Scripture is God's witness to Himself.

2. Holy Scripture, being God's own Word, written by men prepared and superintended by His Spirit, is of infallible divine authority in all matters upon which it touches: it is to be believed, as God's instruction, in all that it affirms; obeyed, as God's command, in all that it requires; embraced, as God's pledge, in all that it promises.

3. The Holy Spirit, Scripture's divine Author, both authenticates it to us by His inward witness and opens our minds to understand its meaning.

4. Being wholly and verbally God-given, Scripture is without error or fault in all its teaching, no less in what it states about God's acts in creation, about the events of world history, and about its own literary origins under God, than in its witness to God's saving grace in individual lives.

5. The authority of Scripture is inescapably impaired if this total divine inerrancy is in any way limited or disregarded, or made relative to a view of truth contrary to the Bible's own; and such lapses bring serious loss to both the individual and the Church.

ARTICLES OF AFFIRMATION AND DENIAL

Article I

We affirm that the Holy Scriptures are to be received as the authoritative Word of God.

We deny that the Scriptures receive their authority from the Church, tradition, or any other human source.

Article II

We affirm that the Scriptures are the supreme written norm by which God binds the conscience, and that the authority of the Church is subordinate to that of Scripture.

We deny that Church creeds, councils, or declarations have authority greater than or equal to the authority of the Bible.

Article III

We affirm that the written Word in its entirety is revelation given by God.

We deny that the Bible is merely a witness to revelation, or only becomes revelation in encounter, or depends on the responses of men for its validity.

Article IV

We affirm that God who made mankind in His image has used language as a means of revelation.

We deny that human language is so limited by our creatureliness that it is rendered inadequate as a vehicle for divine revelation. We further deny that the corruption of human culture and language through sin has thwarted God's work of inspiration.

Article V

We affirm that God's revelation in the Holy Scriptures was progressive.

We deny that later revelation, which may fulfil earlier revelation, ever corrects or contradicts it. We further deny that any normative revelation has been given since the completion of the New Testament writings.

Article VI

We affirm that the whole of Scripture and all its parts, down to the very words of the original, were given by divine inspiration.

We deny that the inspiration of Scripture can rightly be affirmed of the whole without the parts, or of some parts but not the whole.

Article VII

We affirm that inspiration was the work in which God by His Spirit, through human writers, gave us His Word. The origin of Scripture is divine. The mode of divine inspiration remains largely a mystery to us.

We deny that inspiration can be reduced to human insight, or to heightened states of consciousness of any kind.

Article VIII

We affirm that God in His Work of inspiration utilized the distinctive personalities and literary styles of the writers whom He had chosen and prepared.

We deny that God, in causing these writers to use the very words that He chose, overrode their personalities.

Article IX

We affirm that inspiration, though not conferring omniscience, guaranteed true and trustworthy utterance on all matters of which the Biblical authors were moved to speak and write.

We deny that the finitude or fallenness of these writers, by necessity or otherwise, introduced distortion or falsehood into God's Word.

Article X

We affirm that inspiration, strictly speaking, applies only to the autographic text of Scripture, which in the providence of God can be ascertained from available manuscripts with great accuracy. We further affirm that copies and translations of Scripture are the Word of God to the extent that they faithfully represent the original.

We deny that any essential element of the Christian faith is affected by the absence of the autographs. We further deny that this absence renders the assertion of Biblical inerrancy invalid or irrelevant.

Article XI

We affirm that Scripture, having been given by divine inspiration, is infallible, so that, far from misleading us, it is true and reliable in all the matters it addresses.

We deny that it is possible for the Bible to be at the same time infallible and errant in its assertions. Infallibility and inerrancy may be distinguished, but not separated.

Article XII

We affirm that Scripture in its entirety is inerrant, being free from all falsehood, fraud, or deceit.

We deny that Biblical infallibility and inerrancy are limited to spiritual, religious, or redemptive themes, exclusive of assertions in the fields of history and science. We further deny that scientific hypotheses about earth's history may properly be used to overturn the teaching of Scripture on creation and the flood.

Article XIII

We affirm the propriety of using inerrancy as a theological term with reference to the complete truthfulness of Scripture.

We deny that it is proper to evaluate Scripture according to standards of truth and error that are alien to its usage or purpose. We further deny that inerrancy is negated by Biblical phenomena such as a lack of modern technical precision, irregularities of grammar or spelling, observational descriptions of nature, the reporting of falsehoods, the use of hyperbole and round numbers, the topical arrangement of material, variant selections of material in parallel accounts, or the use of free citations.

Article XIV

We affirm the unity and internal consistency of Scripture.

We deny that alleged errors and discrepancies that have not yet been resolved vitiate the truth of the claims of the Bible.

Article XV

We affirm that the doctrine of inerrancy is grounded in the teaching of the Bible about inspiration.

We deny that Jesus' teaching about Scripture may be dismissed by appeals to accommodation or to any natural limitation of His humanity.

Article XVI

We affirm that the doctrine of inerrancy has been integral to the Church's faith throughout its history.

We deny that inerrancy is a doctrine invented by Scholastic Protestantism, or is a reactionary position postulated in response to negative higher criticism.

Article XVII

We affirm that the Holy Spirit bears witness to the Scriptures, assuring believers of the truthfulness of God's written Word.

We deny that this witness of the Holy Spirit operates in isolation from or against Scripture.

Article XVIII

We affirm that the text of Scripture is to be interpreted by grammatico-historical exegesis, taking account of its literary forms and devices, and that Scripture is to interpret Scripture.

We deny the legitimacy of any treatment of the text or quest for sources lying behind it that leads to relativizing, dehistoricizing, or discounting its teaching, or rejecting its claims to authorship.

Article XIX

We affirm that a confession of the full authority, infallibility, and inerrancy of Scripture is vital to a sound understanding of the whole of the Christian faith. We further affirm that such confession should lead to increasing conformity to the image of Christ.

We deny that such confession is necessary for salvation. However, we further deny that inerrancy can be rejected without grave consequences, both to the individual and to the Church.

Index to significant subjects

These references will take the reader only to the book and chapter (eg 1/3, 4/5) in this series where the more significant references to the subject occur.

Index to significant subjects

Index to significant subjects

Index to significant subjects

Index to main Scripture references

These references will take the reader only to the book and chapter (eg 1/3, 4/5) in this series where the more significant Scripture references occur.

EVIDENCE
for the BIBLE

Clive Anderson and
Brian Edwards

LARGE FORMAT HARDBACK
FULL COLOUR THROUGHOUT
225mm × 275mm
260pp | ISBN 978-1-84625-416-1
REF EFB4161 | £25.00

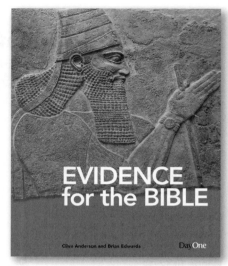

Evidence will surprise and inform you as you turn over the soil of history with the pages of your Bible. The witness of the trowel authenticates and illuminates the people and events, lifting them from the pages of the Book and setting them in the context of time and place. Join us on an exciting journey with this evidence from the past.

Evidence for the Bible can be found in many places, from the Ancient Near East to museums and private collections. Whilst artefacts can never prove the authority of the Bible, they can and do show that the events described in the Bible occurred in time and history.

This book provides a selection of the many items that demonstrate the reliability of the Bible as a historical document.

'Clive Anderson and Brian Edwards have captured the essence of generations of middle-eastern archaeology, historical context and biblical landscape in a quite remarkable way. Their book is accessible, informative and enjoyable. The pictures beautifully complement the text. The Bible comes alive. I warmly and wholeheartedly commend it to everyone who wishes to be a little wiser and better informed about the Book which has formed our culture and is the source of the Christian Faith.'

THE VERY REVD JAMES ATWELL,
Dean of Winchester.

'This is a marvellous introduction to the finds of archaeology that illumine our understanding of the Bible. It helps the reader to see that the biblical events and writings took place within history. When the reader studies the Bible, this book will serve as a wonderful tool to help get at its depth and richness. I highly recommend it.'

DR JOHN D CURRID
Carl McMurray Professor of Old Testament at the Reformed Theological Seminary, Charlotte, USA.

Through the British Museum with the Bible

Clive Anderson and Brian Edwards

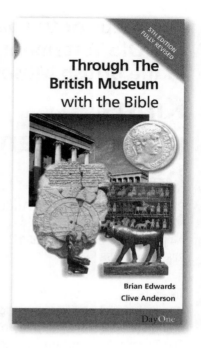

FULL COLOUR TRAVEL GUIDE
128pp | ISBN 978-1-90308-754-6
REF TWBM | £10.00

This guide centres on those items in the British Museum that are related to the history recorded in the Bible. You will be introduced to rulers, empires and cultures that, without the careful work of many scholars, would have been lost for ever. In this guide you have all that you need to make your tour both enjoyable and relevant. The past is brought to light in front of you.

'The British Museum is a great storehouse of treasures from the past; the Bible is the greatest treasure of all. This guide brings them together in a concise way that will help readers to understand more clearly what each has to offer.'

—ALAN MILLARD, *Rankin Professor Emeritus of Hebrew and Ancient Semitic Languages, The University of Liverpool. Formerly Assistant Keeper of Western Asiatic Antiquities at the British Museum.*

'I am delighted that this fine guide is available in a second and fully revised edition. The British Museum is unique worldwide for its collection of antiquities which illustrate Bible times and customs and this guide enables anyone, either alone or with a group, to identify them accurately. It is both reliable and easy to use.'

—DONALD J. WISEMAN, *Professor Emeritus of Assyriology in the University of London, formerly Assistant Keeper in the Egyptian and Western Asiatic Antiquities at the British Museum and President of the British School of Archaeology in Iraq.*

Footsteps of the past: The Old Testament in the British Museum

Kings, pharaohs and bandits

Brian Edwards and Clive Anderson

A4 | 32pp | ISBN 978-1-84625-035-4
REF FPBMOT358 | £3.00

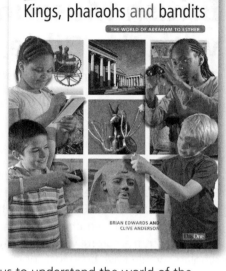

Treasure that is not jewels, bandits' gold, mysterious writing and dead bodies all wrapped up helps us to understand the world of the Old Testament. Here you can see the fantastic Pharaohs, the horrible pictures of the Assyrians, the elegant drinking vessels of the Persians, and the son of a king who conquered the world. With puzzles to solve, pictures to colour and items to find, this book will give you an understanding about a world that has passed but is living in front of your face!

'This book is a good twin to *Romans, Gladiators and Games*, by the same authors. It covers many Bible stories children will know well and points out where artifices mentioned in the Bible can be found in the Museum. It shows how to do hieroglyphics and how bodies were mummified in Egypt—little boys will love that bit. There are plenty of things to do and make at home as well as at the Museum, where there are many things to look for. At home you can make a model of a mummy and turn a box into a coffin to put it in to, among many other things. Included is a recipe for a Middle Eastern drink which looks tasty. I think that there is plenty in this book which would deepen the children's knowledge of Bible events and also keep them happily engaged for hours with the activities and crafts.'

BARBARA STONEHAM, *GoodBookStall Review*

Footsteps of the past: The New Testament in the British Museum

Romans, gladiators and games

Brian Edwards and Clive Anderson

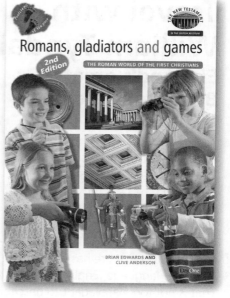

A4 | 32pp | ISBN 978-1-84625-036-1
REF FPBMNT366 | £3.00

Gladiators fighting to the death, cruel emperors who control the lives of millions and marbles you cannot roll—all waiting for you to discover. Step into the exciting world of the first century, see how people lived, worked, played and died. Into this world a new religion was born. See what marks the Christian faith left on the lives of people, and wonder at the change it made to history. Colour in a centurion, find out the size of Diana, discover the lights that people used in the evenings and many more fascinating activities.

'This is a really interesting book. It is a guide book and also an activity book for children, which covers aspects of life in Ancient Rome, from gladiatorial battles to games the children played. It is a companion book to the adult version travel guide *Through the British Museum with the Bible*. It takes children around the various rooms at the Museum showing specific items of interest that children may like such as masks, swords etc. It also explains how some of our words came into being. It is especially good at including lots of activities for children such as how to make a copy of a mask that is in the Museum. But above all, it does this showing where in the Bible these things are mentioned and how the people of Jesus' time would have understood the use of the illustrations, for example lamps or swords. I think most children would learn a lot from the book yet most importantly enjoy while learning.'

BARBARA STONEHAM, *GoodBookStall Review*

Travel with William Tyndale

England's greatest Bible translator

Brian H Edwards

FULL COLOUR TRAVEL GUIDE
128pp | ISBN 978-1-84625-160-3
REF TWWT1603 | £10.00

Melvyn Bragg in 'The Adventure of English' claims that William Tyndale wrote 'the most influential book there has ever been in the history of language, English or any other.' That is not too extravagant to describe the significance of Tyndale's translation into English of the whole of the New Testament and much of the Old from the original Greek and Hebrew. Tyndale is undoubtedly one of the greatest Englishmen ever, and all who speak this language owe him a great debt.

'This is a guide not only to Tyndale's places in England and on the continent, but also to his time, his ideas and his spirit. It is based on meticulous research and profound scholarly insight, whilst remaining very readable and entertaining.'
GUIDO LATRÉ, *University of Louvain*

Grace— amazing grace

Brian H Edwards

304pp | ISBN 978-1-84625-336-2
REF GRACE | £9.00

'Grace is the most beautiful word in our language and the supreme description of God.' With these opening words the author introduces his theme, and in seventeen chapters portrays the grace of God in its vast array. In a popular and penetrating style, the author compels us forward with theology for the heart. This book is firmly theological, warmly devotional and incisively practical.

Brian Edwards questions the commonly accepted positions in 'forgiving grace', provides a robust chapter on 'universal grace' and a moving chapter on 'incarnate grace'. In particular his approach to 'ultimate grace' is an intriguing and fitting conclusion to the whole subject. The questions at the close of each chapter make this an excellent book for small group discussion.

'As Brian Edwards tells us, "Grace encompasses all the great truths of Christianity, for without grace they would have no meaning." He then guides us on a delightful tour that takes us from God's common grace for all mankind to the ultimate grace of heaven for God's people. I have never read anything better on the subject than this superb and sure-footed treatment.'

DR JOHN BLANCHARD, *evangelist, author and Christian apologist*

The Ten Commandments for today

Brian H Edwards

288pp | ISBN 978-1-90308-733-6
REF 10T | £9.00

At a time when the nation's morality is in alarming decline, it is surprising that so little has been written on the Ten Commandments. This modern commentary carefully uncovers their true meaning and incisively applies them to our contemporary society. Probably never in the history of western civilisation have the Ten Commandments been more neglected and therefore more relevant than today.

This book is a superbly written modern commentary on God's changeless laws in today's changing and godless society.

'This book unpacks the crammed meaning of these terse commands, and applies them pointedly to life in a deregulated age.'
ANDREW ANDERSON

'This is a highly readable treatment of a vital subject and can be gratefully recommended."
EVANGELICAL TIMES

'Seldom have I appreciated a book more than this one…'
THE GOSPEL MAGAZINE

GOD'S LITTLE PEOPLE

Brian H Edwards

For every person whose name blazes across the pages of our heritage of history in the large letters of a Tyndale, Bunyan, Wesley, Spurgeon or Lloyd-Jones, there are tens of thousands of "little people" who have courageously and faithfully maintained a stand for the truth and have extended the borders of the Kingdom of God. It is upon these that the Lord builds his church. Fascinating insights from Brian Edwards in these volumes. Scripture index included in each.

Little people in Paul's letters
ISBN 978-1-90308-785-5
REF GLP1 | £5.00

The apostles of Jesus
ISBN: 978-1-90308-794-7 | Day One
Code: GLP2 | £5.00

Little women in the Bible
ISBN: 978-1-84625-025-5
REF GLP3250 | £5.00

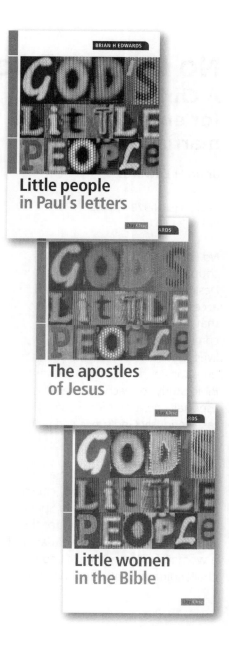

Little people
in Paul's letters

The apostles
of Jesus

Little women
in the Bible

No Longer Two
A Christian guide for engagement and marriage

Brian H Edwards

192pp | ISBN 978-1-84625-173-3
REF NL2 | £8.00

No Longer Two is a guide for couples preparing for marriage. Designed in a contemporary and accessible style, it faces the issues that will confront two people committing the whole of their lives together. With preparation questions and a brief but relevant Bible Study for each chapter, it is especially designed for those who take seriously God's revealed plan for marriage.

No Longer Two has become a standard handbook used by church leaders in many countries (a Spanish translation is also available) for the vital ministry of preparing a man and a woman for the most exciting and challenging adventure of their lives.

'We have used *No Longer Two* preparing Christians and non Christians for marriage for nearly fifteen years. Thank you.'
DAVID AND DIANA, *England*

'We bought Brian and Barbara Edwards' book two years after we were married and found that its practical problem-solving strategies and insightful candidness made us wish we'd had it right from the beginning!'
MARKO AND MIRIAM, *Australia*

'No Longer Two was a marvellous tool to stimulate discussion and decisions on various issues that could potentially become obstacles later on in married life.'
FRANCOIS AND SHARON, *South Africa*

'Quite simply one of the best books on the market today on the subject of marriage.'
THE MONTHLY RECORD, Scotland

Additional commendations

'This superb series provides a set of quality tools, enabling every thoughtful Christian to know how to answer the Bible's critics and grow in their own confidence and appreciation of God's living and enduring Word. Packed with valuable factual information, detailed documentation, wide-ranging references and penetrating reasoning, not a sceptical stone is left unturned and not a critical argument goes unanswered.

Here is a comprehensive and greatly needed resource, which deserves to be required reading for every believer as we seek to live by God's inerrant revelation and present its message with authenticity to an unbelieving world. I could not commend the series more warmly.'

DAVID JACKMAN, *author, former President of the Proclamation Trust and founder of the Cornhill Training Course*

'A superb collection, readable and reliable, with lots of footnotes to check out the material presented. A terrific resource for both believers and those seeking faith. Students at Moorlands will love this series. Highly recommended!'

DR STEVE BRADY, *Principal, Moorlands College, Christchurch*

'*All you need to know about the Bible* blends apologetics, history and biblical studies to produce this important and hugely enjoyable series. It provides the reader with a mental landscape within which a confident and intelligent love for the Bible can be nurtured. It is a tour de force and a marvellous gift to the church in our secular age. I could not commend it more warmly or enthusiastically.'

RICHARD CUNNINGHAM, *Director, Universities and Colleges Christian Unions*

'Accessible throughout, these comprehensive introductory accounts of Scripture will be of immense value to everyone who reads them. They go far beyond a simple introduction and probe deeply into the nature of the Bible as the faultless Word of God, considering and answering a full range of criticisms. Moreover, Brian writes in a manner that will benefit the newest Christian. I hope his work receives the widest possible readership.'

DR ROBERT LETHAM, *Professor of Systematic and Historical Theology, Union School of Theology, Wales*

Book 2: Big claims from a unique book **143**

Additional commendations

'This series of attractive, accessible introductions offers a feast of wisdom and insight into the origins and accuracy of the Bible. When navigating the complex issues surrounding ancient texts and modern translations, here is an excellent place to begin—a helpful guide to the basics of history, archaeology and manuscript evidence. Most importantly, the series encourages us to delight afresh in the truthfulness, sufficiency and authority of God's Word. These volumes will be of assistance to every Bible student.'

DR ANDREW ATHERSTONE, *Latimer Research Fellow, Wycliffe Hall, Oxford*

'The overwhelming strength of Brian's comprehensive series is that it provides ordinary Christians with confidence in the authority of the Bible. Brian has the skill to make this subject accessible without simplification or omission. What a great resource for Christians, equipping us to be on the front foot when it comes to defending the Bible against its many detractors!'

ADRIAN REYNOLDS, *author, local church pastor and Training Director of the Fellowship of Independent Evangelical Churches*

'Each one of these books is a valuable guide to the teaching and historical reliability of the Bible. Together, the set builds a compelling case for the authority of Scripture as the very words of God with life-changing power. A wealth of material in readable style, it is a rich resource, giving fresh confidence in the reliability and authority of the Scriptures.'

BILL JAMES, *Principal, The London Seminary*

'Like a jeweller turning a diamond so that every facet flashes with light, Brian holds up God's Word so that its perfections shine. Although my views differ from his on Bible translations, these books serve well to answer helpfully numerous objections, confirm faith, and wisely guide in profitable reading of the Word.'

DR JOEL R. BEEKE, *President, Puritan Reformed Theological Seminary, Grand Rapids, Michigan*